THE GLOBAL HISTORY SERIES

Leften Stavrianos, *Northwestern University*
General Editor

This series aims to present history in global perspective, going beyond national or regional limitations, and dealing with overriding
trends and forces. The various collections of original materials span
the globe, range from prehistoric times to the present, and include
anthropology, economics, political science, and religion, as well as
history.

Joseph R. Levenson, the editor of this volume, is Sather Professor
of History at the University of California, Berkeley. He is the author
of *Liang Ch'i-ch'ao and the Mind of Modern China* and the trilogy,
Confucian China and Its Modern Fate.

Also in the Global History Series

EUROPEAN EXPANSION
AND THE COUNTER-EXAMPLE
OF ASIA, 1300-1600

EUROPEAN EXPANSION
AND THE COUNTER-EXAMPLE
OF ASIA, 1300-1600

EDITED BY JOSEPH R. LEVENSON

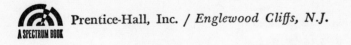
Prentice-Hall, Inc. / *Englewood Cliffs, N.J.*
A SPECTRUM BOOK

ACKNOWLEDGMENTS

The editor wishes to thank Mr. Henry Talbot, Senior, Lecturer in Geography at the University of Hong Kong, for his generous assistance with maps, and Miss Ann Hsu of the University of California, Berkeley, for general assistance.

CONTENTS

MAPS

A comparison of circular maps from Europe and East Asia is revealing.
Both seem cosmological rather than primarily cartographic: the Christian
significance of the Ebstorf map, with its iconographic element and Jerusalem
at the center, is clear, while the Sino-Korean map perhaps harks back to a
Buddhist "mandala" conception. What distinguishes these maps from each
other is not so much the respective world-views behind them, but their
dates. When such maps had long been superseded in Europe they were being reprinted in Asia, where the early-modern global-expansion syndrome
did not come into being.

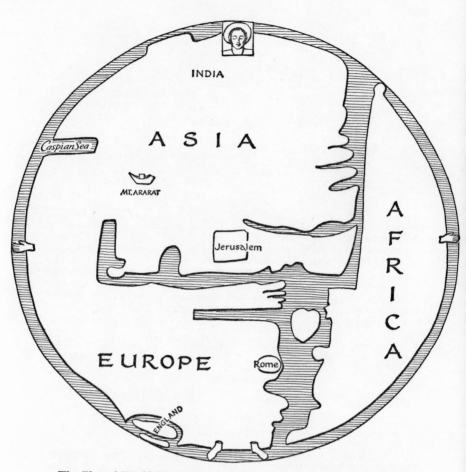

INDIA

A S I A

Caspian Sea

MT. ARARAT

Jerusalem

A F R I C A

EUROPE

Rome

ENGLAND

The Ebstorf World Map (above), c. 1235, is probably the work of Gervase of Tilbury. It measures, overall, 140.9 × 140.2 inches in 30 sheets of parchment. This is a very large and rather late example of a type of world map common in Medieval Europe and known as a "T & O" map from the circular shape and the shape of the central sea (in this case one bar of the "T" is missing). The orientation was with east to the top (hence the origin of the term "orientation"). The religious figure (head at the top, hands at each side, feet at the bottom) makes it clear how this map served as an altarpiece for the Benedictine monastery at Ebstorf near Ulzen on the Luneburg Heath in Germany. This could perhaps be described as a "cosmological map" giving a schematic view of the terrestrial part of the universe as it was visualized at that time. (Shown here is a much simplified version.)

References: Leo Bagrow, *History of Cartography* (London, 1964), Plate E; E. Sommerbrodt, *Die Ebstorfer Weltkarte* (Hannover, 1891); W. Rosien, *Die Ebstorfer Weltkarte* (Hannover, 1952).

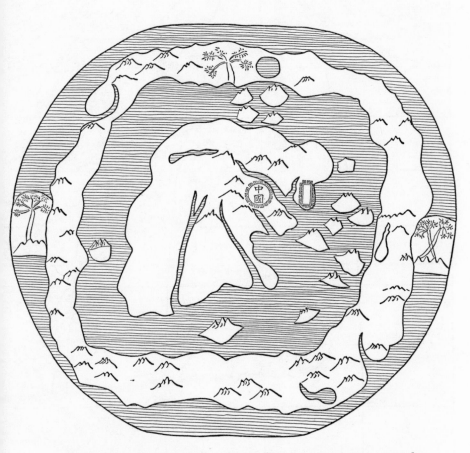

Circular World Map from Korea (above). This is a type of map commonly found in old Korean atlases. The example shown is a simplification of a map printed about 1712. Analysis of the place-names (only the "Middle Kingdom," i.e., China, has been retained here) shows heavy reliance on the Chinese classic "Shan Hai Ching"; certainly there are no place-names of later than the eleventh century A.D. It seems clear that this type of map originated in China. The similarity to the European "T & O" maps has suggested to Needham that there may be a common origin.

References: M. Courant, *Bibliographie Coréenne* (Paris, 1894), Vol. II, Plate X (opposite p. 480); Hirosi Nakamura, *Old Chinese World Maps Preserved by the Koreans* (Imago Mundi, 1947), pp. 3-22; Joseph Needham, *Science and Civilization in China* (Cambridge, 1959), Vol. III, 565-568, 588 (also see Bibliography).

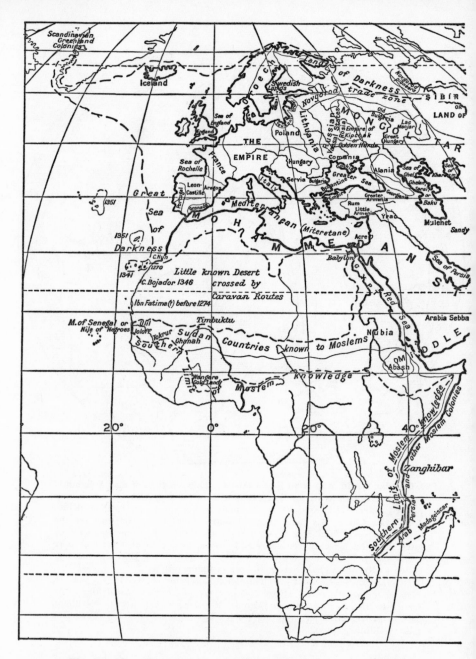

The World as Known to Western Europeans About A.D. 1260-1360, the century of the Mongol Eurasian empire, the background to Europe's expan-

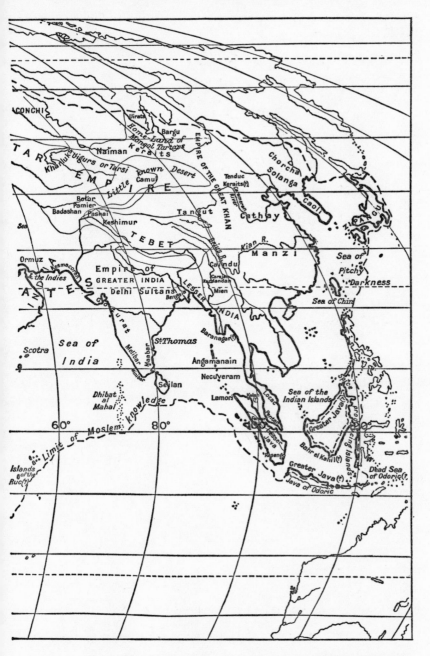

CONCHI

Uirata

Bargu

Home-Land of
Mongol Tartars

Camul

Keraits

Naiman

Kharluk Uigurs or Tarsi

Little brown Desert

TAR EMPIRE

Betor
Pamier
Badashan
Pashai

Keshimur

TEBET

Ormuz

Kesmacoran

Sea

& the Indies

ZTES

Empire of
GREATER INDIA

Delhi Sultans

Guzurat

Meilbar

Maabar

Hunter

Seilan

Scotra

Sea of
India

Dhibat
al
Mahal

Islands
of the
Ruc(?)

EMPIRE OF THE GREAT KHAN

Tenduc
Keraits(?)

Caramoran River

Tangut

Pulis R.

Caindu

Caragian
Zardandan

Bengala

Mien

LESSER

INDIA

St Thomas

Baranagar

Angamanain

Necuveram

Lamori

Kian R.

Manzi

Cathay

Chorcha

Solanga

Caoli

ZIPANGU

Sea of
Pitchy
Darkness

Sea of Chin

Kelah

Locac

Pentan

Ferlec

Basman

Java

Greater Java (?)

Java of Odoric

Rasengo

Bahr el Kahil(?)

Sea of the
Indian Islands

spice producing Islands

Greater Java

Dead Sea
of Odoric(?)

60°   Moslem   knowledge   80°

Limit of

sion by sea. (From C. Raymond Beazeley, *The Dawn of Modern Geography* [Oxford: The Clarendon Press, 1906], Vol. III. Reprinted by permission.)

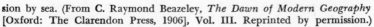

GENERAL INTRODUCTION

. . . At the close of the fifteenth century Europe was only one of four Eurasian centers of civilization, and by no means the most prominent. By the end of the eighteenth century it had gained control of the ocean routes, organized an immensely profitable worldwide commerce, and conquered vast territories in the Americas and India and Siberia. Thus in the perspective of world history the period stands out as a period of transition from the regional isolation of the pre-1492 era to the European global hegemony of the nineteenth century; and for this reason, not because of a narrowly "Europacentric" view of the past, Europe as the main center of innovation and decision remains prominent. But the aspects of European history which receive emphasis are inevitably different. In terms of their global significance, the battles that stand out will not be those, such as Pavia (1525), which loom so large in the common run of history books, but Mohacs (1526), Lepanto (1571), Itamarca (1640); and it is significant that two of the three were naval battles. The defeat of the Turks at Lepanto, in particular, marked the shift of the axis of European history away from the Mediterranean to the Atlantic seaboard in the West and thus a significant stage in the history of European expansion. This expansion, as the distinguishing feature of the period—in the medieval centuries Europe had been hemmed in by the expanding civilizations of the Near East—is from a universal point of view the central theme. The first question it raises—a question which has not hitherto been systematically studied, though it takes us deep into European history —is what the roots of expansion were, or why it started from Europe and not from one of the other Eurasian centers of civilization.*

What I call the phenomenon of Europe has, when seen in the scale of world history, a number of completely original and distinctive features. Take, for example, the following:

* Geoffrey Barraclough, "Universal History," in H. P. R. Finberg, ed., *Approaches to History: A Symposium* (London: Routledge and Kegan Paul Ltd., 1962), p. 104. Reprinted by permission of the publisher.

1

1. Europe discovered the whole of the earth, and nobody ever came and discovered Europe.
2. Europe has held sway on all the continents in succession, and up till now has never been ruled by any foreign power.
3. Europe has produced a civilization which is being imitated by the whole world, while the converse has never happened.†

When European vessels, beginning in the fifteenth century, finally conquered the oceans, the world stood at the turning of modern history, the turning toward the world history of our own day. Why was it Europe that forced the world to be a world—why did the force (military, political, economic, cultural) spread out from the West, not from the East? This book itself is meant to exemplify a world, a world of discourse in which the reasons why Asia failed to expand suggest finally why Europe expanded. It is the relevance of different historical dynamics to one another, not the details of historical relations between different areas, that we seek to discern. Asian history is brought to bear on European, to explain how Europe, from the sixteenth to the twentieth centuries, came to bear down on Asia.

That story is a familiar one. The Portuguese led the way, probing down the west coast of Africa. Then, under Vasco da Gama, they rounded the Cape of Good Hope and reached Calicut, on the West coast of India, in 1498. Led by Albuquerque, the Portuguese established a string of garrisons and trading posts in Southeast Asia, and in 1516 a Portuguese ship anchored at the great southeast China port of Canton. In the same century the Spanish took the Philippines. By the end of the seventeenth century the Dutch and British had effectively ended the commercial reign of Portugal in the East, and the stage was set for the East India companies of northern Europe—English, Dutch, French, Danish, Swedish—to implicate Europe deeply in East Asian economic life. Great Britain and Holland established their political sway in South and Southeast Asia, laying the ground for the political and cultural pressure on China which in the nineteenth century would reach such devastating proportions. Japan lay over the horizon, out of reach after the early seventeenth century (except for desultory, severely controlled Dutch trading missions), but not reaching out itself until after the Meiji Restoration of 1868. Agents and patients— from the early modern period down to almost our own day, Eu-

† Denis de Rougemont, *The Meaning of Europe* (London: Sidgwick & Jackson Ltd., 1963), p. 12. Reprinted by permission of Sidgwick & Jackson Ltd., Stein and Day, Inc., and Editions de la Baconniere.

rope played the active role while Asia, almost passively, endured.

Thus were established the conditions that make statements like Barraclough's and de Rougemont's (the epigrams for this Introduction) comprehensible. De Rougemont is the more truculent, reacting, it seems, to a certain shift of interest from Europe (the classical subject for Europeans) to other parts of the world. We shall see him later, distinguishing a European "spirit" from any other. Barraclough sounds the more neutral tone of inquiry, with its note of comparison, not assertion.

Max Weber sounded this note earlier in the century, as he pressed his inquiry into the origins of the "spirit of capitalism." Writing about Confucianism and (less successfully) about Taoism in China, Weber was taking the long way home to the European Reformation, and to his thesis that the spread of the "Protestant ethic" was crucial for the rise of modern capitalism. Despite social conditions in China that seemed (to Weber) favorable to modern capitalist developments, such developments did not occur, and Weber saw the Confucian ethic as the inhibiting factor. Since Confucianism and Puritanism were in sharp contrast at several critical points—the conception of the aesthetic value and self-sufficiency of the Confucian "princely man" versus the Puritan "vocation," the Confucian ideal of adjustment to the world versus the Puritan ideal of the rational transformation of the world, etc.—Weber concluded that the negative influence of Confucianism in China, with respect to capitalism, corroborated his theory of the positive influence, in this regard, of Puritanism in Europe. (Weber included studies of ancient Judaism and religions of India, too, in his *Gesammelte Aufsätze zur Religionssoziologie* [*Collected Essays on the Sociology of Religion*, Tubingen, 1922-23], to buttress his thesis there on "The Protestant Ethic and the Spirit of Capitalism.")

Up to a point Joseph Needham, in *Science and Civilisation in China* (seven volumes projected), examines a theme like Weber's. Just as Weber dwells on the early proto-capitalist activity in China, Needham describes the impressive record of early Chinese science. From the vantage point of, say, the middle of the thirteenth century, one might very well, on Weber's and Needham's showing, expect that China would lead the world into the modern age of capitalism and the hegemony of science and technology. This, of course, proved not to be the case, and Weber, as we have suggested (Needham is more ambiguous here), used the evidence of *potential* in China to help him form a hypothesis about *realization* somewhere else. Because Europe was *not* the obvious candidate for priority, comparisons had to be made with other well-qualified candidates; comparisons might isolate the crucial factors in development and abortiveness: the stimuli in Europe, the depressants in Asia.

The colonial expansion of Europe, too, is a modern theme on the grand scale, like the development of capitalism or science and technology. And here, too, the Asian potential was striking, but failed to be realized. Why, for describing a trend in non-Western histories, have the terms "modernization" and "Westernization" contended? "Westernization" may well be rejected, but it has certainly been proposed. It would be whimsical to propose the theme of the "Easternization" of Europe, meaning cultural "modernization." Why should this be so? In the fifteenth century, when Europe, led by Portugal, was poised to press conclusively into Asia, it was not clear that this had to inaugurate "the age of Vasco da Gama." * Might we not have entered, instead, "the age of Cheng Ho" (see below)? To suggest why not, let us canvas (in the comparative mode of the science and capitalism problems) hypotheses from several realms of possible explanation: technology, religion, "spirit," and social structure.

1 / THE ROOTS OF EUROPE'S INTEREST IN ASIA

Before there could be anything to explain about Western expansion and Asian non-expansion, a serious Western interest in Asia had to be generated. It was not simply given from the beginning, just as an Asian interest in Europe had not always existed. Europe and Asia—eastern Asia, especially—were indifferent to each other for a long time. The following selection indicates why this was so.

Little was known in Europe about Asia until the thirteenth century, when missionaries and merchants made their way into the interior of the continent. At that time the scant information about the Orient was limited to what had been handed down in the treatises and accounts of late antiquity, which retained some vague ideas and many fables about the men and things to be found in

---

* Term coined by the late Indian scholar and diplomat, K. M. Panikkar, to describe the centuries of European hegemony in the East. Da Gama, as we have seen, was the Portuguese navigator who reached India in 1498, initiating the European expansion into Asian waters.

From Leonardo Olschki, *Marco Polo's Asia* (Berkeley and Los Angeles: University of California Press, 1960), pp. 40-46. Reprinted by permission of the publisher. Footnotes omitted.

those distant lands. The wonders of India are a commonplace in classical texts. In the verses of Virgil and Claudian there lived the memory of the East, the mythical Seres, from which came the silk that was so precious, and about which Pliny, Ammianus Marcellinus, and other late Latin authors, repeated what Ptolemy had known about it before them.

But all this sparse, indeterminate information preserved for centuries its erudite, literary character without being changed or renewed by any direct mercantile, military, maritime, political, or religious experience. The Byzantines had learned more about it, through their political and commercial contacts with the Persians and Turks of western Asia; and the account of China given by Theophylact Simocatta, a Greek chronicler of the seventh century, the last Western author before Marco to describe the land and its customs, is famous.

The Mohammedan expansion that followed soon afterward, with the conquest of the Middle East as far as the borders of India and Eastern Turkestan, placed a compact barrier between East and West, preventing the exchange of information and goods that would have allowed some reports—however vague and infrequent—about the various nations and civilizations to pass in both directions. It is of course true that this same Mohammedan invasion of the first half of the seventh century drove Nestorian missions and communities from Syria to China, where they settled in various centers of the empire; but the result was an even more decisive separation between Asian and Western Christianity, and an increase in mutual ignorance, rather than common contacts and heightened curiosity.

The Crusades, which led large numbers from every quarter of Europe to the western edge of Asia, did not change the situation. Their great chroniclers do not seem to have directed their geographical, ethnographical, or historical curiosity beyond the lands won back to Christianity; indeed for the intelligent and learned Fulcher of Chartres, a historian of the First Crusade, the world of the fabulous wonders of Asia begins immediately after those fragments of the Holy Land and the Levant that had been liberated by the Christian armies, and he gives not one single hint of even the most superficial experience of the lands and peoples of the Middle East.

This indifference toward all aspects of exotic nature and life, at this time and for a long time to come, embraced the whole of the Mohammedan world, from the Atlantic to the China Sea, of whose peoples, customs, and ideas the Christian community remained ignorant almost throughout the Middle Ages. The scanty data offered by the numerous itineraries of the Holy Land reveal the limits of the geographical curiosity of the medieval mind, which never extended beyond the Biblical and hagiographical interest of the travelers or beyond the regions visited by them.

The exchange of goods between East and West contributed very little to the expansion of these geographical horizons, restricted by both experience and tradition. Textiles, gems, pearls, and spices were for centuries imported into Europe, but little was known about their lands or origin. Indeed, these limited commercial relations remained indirect, until Marco Polo's time, without there ever having remained any record of a personal exchange of goods between the two great areas of production and consumption into which the Euro-Asian world was then divided: the one, dominated by a Mohammedan monopoly of commerce, extending from Alexandria in Egypt to the China Sea, from the banks of the Volga to the northern boundaries of India; the other, Mediterranean and Christian, increasingly activated by the competition in arms and commerce that existed between the Italian maritime republics.

These two areas into which the Old World was divided during the Middle Ages were so tenaciously separated and autonomous that nothing seems to have been known in the West about the great Asian experiences of the Mohammedan peoples. Their flourishing medieval geographical literature, which had begun in the ninth century in Mesopotamia and Persia and had extended to Sicily and Spain in an uninterrupted succession of scientific and popular treatises, dealt with all the lands and areas then known to them and included works of lasting historical and practical value. It would be fruitless to search for a reflection of this in Western literature, which had, however, from the twelfth century onward, gathered much scientific and philosophical knowledge from the translators at Toledo and Palermo.

Geography evidently did not form part of the interests of those centuries, in which other fields of human knowledge and activity, for example medicine and astrology, were pre-eminent in the intellectual activity of the West. Hence, all that existed beyond the limits of the Christian world entered the kingdom of fancy; even the goods that came from these inaccessible lands were from regions beyond belief. It would therefore be a mistake to think that the exchange of commercial goods also implied an exchange of culture and ideas. Thus, whereas Arab geographical treatises abound in information, both true and false, about India, Central

Asia, and the Far East, the whole of medieval didactic literature, until halfway through the thirteenth century, does not offer any empirical contribution to the mass of traditional, erudite, and literary information in which it abounded.

Brunetto Latini's *Trésor* affords ample proof. This work was compiled about the year 1260, at the time when Niccolò and Maffeo Polo, Marco's father and uncle, began their first transcontinental journey, which was to lead them from the Venetian emporium at Soldaia (modern Sudak) in the Crimea to the court of the Great Khan Kublai on the borders of Cathay. When he treats of that distant land's inhabitants and its best-known product, silk, Ser Brunetto repeats what Pliny and other ancient writers, who were unaware of the nature and origin of this precious cloth, have to say about it. In fact, we read in this famous work that

> beyond all inhabited places we find men called Scir, or Seres, who by a water process make a woolen cloth from the leaves and barks of trees, wherewith they clothe their bodies. And they are mild and peaceful with one another, and they refuse the company of others. Our merchants, however, cross one of their rivers, and find on the banks of this river all manner of goods that can be found there; and, without any parleying, they look at one another, and with their eyes give the price of each thing. And, when they have seen it, they take away what they want of it and leave payment for it in that same spot. In this way do they sell their merchandise; nor will they have anything to do with ours.

Thus wrote Brunetto at a time when the silkworm had already been introduced in the West for some centuries past, and silken cloths were made up in the Levant, in Sicily, the Aegean Islands, and Spain, a country visited by him. The Italian silk-goods trade had already become concentrated in the north, especially at Lucca, Venice, and in Lombardy. No other document expresses more eloquently the contrast that still existed between popular, didactic information and practical life. Nor would it be possible to find a clearer expression of the mystery which then surrounded the origin of the most valuable Oriental merchandise, although this trade extended uninterruptedly from one end of the Old World to the other.

The ancient fable of silent merchants symbolizes a truth not generally recognized, namely, that an exchange of goods does not necessarily imply an exchange of culture. The tradesmen of Imperial Rome imported from the Far East silken cloths that were worth their weight in gold, but they had no exact idea either of their origin or of the methods of production. Henceforth, and throughout the Middle Ages, it was possible, as in the text quoted, to describe silk as a vegetable product taken from trees and then processed like flax or hemp. Evidently, until Marco Polo's times the commercial activity between the various regions of the earth was not accompanied by a comparable desire to know their peoples and products, apart from what was to be found in the most authoritative sources of ancient knowledge and experience—which was little enough.

In fact, it may be supposed that it was the Western merchants themselves who kept alive the fables about the distant lands from which their goods originated, thus surrounding their offerings with an air of mystery that made them still more precious and desirable; so much so, that pearls, spices, and precious stones, apart from their intrinsic worth, had not only the quality of rarity, but seemed also to possess the therapeutic and magical qualities attributed to them by Latin and vernacular texts of venerable tradition and renewed by the authority of famous contemporary authors. These treatises represent the stationary basis of medieval culture, both learned and popular, in which we still find information and doctrines that date from the Hellenistic period and which no direct experience of Oriental life had ever succeeded in altering. The fact is that all this didactic literature, which comes down from Pliny, Solinus, Pomponius Mela, Isidore of Seville, and their Greek and Asian sources, did not offer to medieval culture one single statement that corresponded to the reality of Oriental life and its geo-ethnographic environment.

In the same way, these Mediterranean shores marked, at that time and for some centuries to come, the western limits of the experiences of peoples at the other end of the earth. For the Chinese and their noteworthy geographical literature the world of fables began on the borders of the Christian world, of which, in spite of the Nestorian colonies which flourished at various times in their territory, there is no definite trace in any of their books. For these Orientals the West is a mythical or eschatological world, beyond the confines of human experience and the range of common curiosity, which, as in Europe, was satisfied with fables as far as these distant regions were concerned. The peoples of the Far East were also unable to penetrate the Mohammedan continental barrier, in spite of the fact that trade and contacts by land and sea formed a part of normal medieval Asian life.

Hence, before missionaries and merchants assumed the twofold function of informants to both the West and the East, that is to say, before the middle of the thirteenth century, when the making of an Asiatic empire that extended from Korea to Poland broke the cultural supremacy and commercial monopoly of the Mohammedans, the little that remained of reciprocal intellectual curiosity was kept alive mainly by fables that were consecrated by literary tradition and clichés and by age-old habits of thought and teaching. Thus, all that was commonly known in Europe about the lands of Islam and the pagans living beyond the narrow limits of geographical experience was for the most part taken from the exploits of Alexander the Great, which from the eleventh century onward dominated in various poetic and fictional forms the Western accounts of the Orient.

"Missionaries and merchants . . .": Olschki refers primarily to Franciscans and Marco Polo. They came to the Far East in the thirteenth century, in a time of Mongol hegemony, when the conquests of Genghis Khan and his successors had fashioned a virtual "Pax Mongolica" from the Volga and Mediterranean to the Pacific.

Despite the threat of the Mongols to Europe, the official Christian attitude was one of friendly overtures, not hostility. There was only one suggestion of a crusade against the invaders. In the early thirteenth century Pope Gregory IX promised the Queen of Georgia that those who took the cross against the "Tartars" would be granted the same indulgences as pilgrims to the Holy Land. Basically, however, the Mongols commended themselves to Christians because the former were buffeting Muslims. To optimists, this seemed to indicate that Christianity might commend itself to Mongols, and the Church was encouraged by the knowledge that tolerance, and in some cases even patronage, had been extended to Christians in the conquered lands. In 1245 the Franciscan John of Plano Carpini was sent by Pope Innocent IV to make contact with the Great Khan at Caracoram, about a hundred miles south of Lake Baikal, north of the Gobi Desert. From then until the fall of the Mongol dynasty of Yüan in China in 1368, Franciscans worked in the Far East, especially in China; the greatest of them, John of Montecorvino (d. 1330), was consecrated Archbishop of Peking, Primate of the East, in 1308.

In 1271 Marco Polo set out for China with his father and uncle, who were Venetian merchants. Twenty years later, after a career in Kublai Khan's bureaucracy, he left China at last, and in 1298, as a prisoner-of-war in Genoa, he dictated the extraordinary story of his great adventure. Marco's straightforward account, together with the many Franciscan reports (generally more exuberant and less informative) brought a new fever for the East to Europe, and the first hard knowledge. All this lay in the background of Portugal's Prince Henry the Navigator and the crowning (though misdirected) achievement of Columbus. The evidence is plain in the Catalan Atlas, a series of maps appearing in 1375, extremely important in the annals of exploration. It portrays the Far Eastern world in the light of information from these missionaries and Marco Polo. The semicircular curve of the coastline is shown, and the cities immortalized by Marco are all there—Cambaluc (Peking), Zayton (Ch'uanchow), Quinsay (Hangchow), and others.

And so the stage was set for the voyages of discovery, European voyages that discovered America, rediscovered Asia, and changed the world. In these few paragraphs we have touched on the religious motif, the spirit of adventure, and the impulse to commerce, themes we shall dwell on later. Before any of these could be indulged in any sustained fashion, to bring Europe to Asia in force, there had to be the technical capacity. Was it this capacity that made the basic difference, and determined the direction—west to east—in which power and influence would flow for so long?

I / TECHNOLOGY

By the time the Portuguese, leading the parade, sailed to India, Indonesia, and China, the Chinese had developed the technical ability to cross their paths on the ocean routes toward Europe. If there was no parade to Europe, inferior Asian technology could not be the ultimate reason.

The following group of extracts tells something of Chinese achievements at sea, up to the coming of sea-borne Europeans to the Far East.

2 / CHINESE NAVAL CAPACITY BY THE MID-FIFTEENTH CENTURY

The Development of Chinese Navigation

[The fourth century A.D. marked the appearance of] Chinese long-distance navigation, [which by] the thirteenth reach[ed] full development. Chinese ships sailed to Penang in Malaya about 350 and Ceylon at the end of the fourth century, by the fifth they were probably coming to the mouth of the Euphrates in Iraq and calling at Aden. Ammianus Marcellinus refers to Chinese merchandise at the annual fair of Batanea on the Euphrates around 360. Such contacts seem to have continued until about 900, when a decline set in. Prisoners from the Talas River returned home from the Gulf in 762 in Chinese junks. About 850 Sulaiman the Merchant refers to the port of Siraf on its north coast as a terminus of Chinese shipping.

Now came the rise of the Islamic Arab shipmasters. In 758 they were strong enough to burn and loot Canton, just a century after

From Joseph Needham, *Science and Civilization in China,* Vol. 1, *Introductory Orientations* (Cambridge: Cambridge University Press, 1954), pp. 179-80. Reprinted by permission of the publisher. Footnotes omitted.

the first Arab embassy to China (651). In the ninth century they habitually circumnavigated Malaya, frequenting Kuangtung in considerable numbers and establishing "colonies" or "factories" there, especially at Canton (Khanfu) and Hangchow (Khanzai), as their predecessors the Syrians and Graeco-Egyptians had done be-

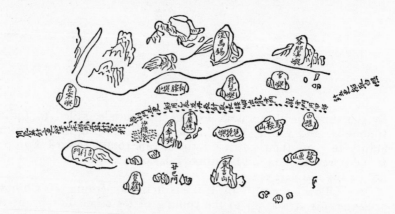

A Chinese sea-chart by Mao Yuan-I, 1629 (derived from Mao K'un) showing Singapore and adjacent islands. Sea-charts had long been used in China alongside land-maps, and the familiarity of Chinese seamen with distant Asian harbors was noted by Marco Polo. Two of the provinces described by him, Ania and Toloman, are taken to be the northeastern point of Asia and the coast of Alaska, and the Gulf of Anian to be the present Bering Strait. (The name Anian is probably Aniva, which is Japanese for the strait separating the island of Sakhalin from the mainland.) The Chinese in fact knew the coasts to the northeast as far as Sakhalin, and possibly even further; and later European missionaries were to use the old Chinese maps of Sakhalin. The routes to the south and west were equally well known in China.

Between 1402 and 1433 seven large naval expeditions despatched by the Ming emperors visited the Malay Archipelago and the Indian Ocean. One expedition went as far as the Red Sea, and an envoy went on from there to Mecca. At the same time, Ma-huan compiled a chart of the voyage. It is said that this was greatly influenced by Arab sea-charts, but this cannot be verified because we have no Arab sea-charts. Ma-huan's sea-chart in its turn influenced later maps, such as those of Mao K'un, who wrote a long treatise, "The Necessity of coastal defense" (1562), containing many maps [including the above]. Ma-K'un's chart showed the whole of the coastal region from Amoy to the Strait of Ormuz, at the entrance to the Persian Gulf. By this time there was also a similar coastal chart of China itself, i.e. the region north of Amoy.

[Illustration and text from Leo Bagrow, *History of Cartography* (revised and enlarged by R. A. Skelton) (London: C. A. Watts & Co., Ltd., 1964). Reprinted by permission.]

fore them, on a much lesser scale, in the third. The Arabs also knew Korea (Sila) and Japan (Wakwak). Huzzayin and Hourani have described this Arab trade in much detail, and Ferrand has collected the texts of Arabic merchants and travelers relative to eastern and southeastern Asia in translated form. This was the time (tenth to thirteenth centuries) for which we have the most important Chinese accounts of maritime commerce and navigation, especially the *Chu Fan Chih* (Records of Foreign Peoples) by Chao Ju-Kua. . . .

* * *

After the end of the twelfth century Arab navigation in Pacific waters gave place to Chinese, and in the fifteenth there came the short-lived period of Chinese maritime supremacy under the Ming dynasty. . . . This again brought Chinese sea-going junks to Borneo, the Philippines, Ceylon, Malabar and even East Africa. Finally, the Portuguese explorations at the beginning of the sixteenth century opened the modern era.

The Naval Feats of Cheng Ho

The Missions of the Yung-lo Reign in the Ming Dynasty

In 1368 a native Chinese dynasty, the Ming, received the Mandate of Heaven, and after a century and a half of alien rule a true son of Han ascended the Dragon Throne. A burst of diplomatic activity followed. It took the form of a grandiose series of naval expeditions designed to announce to the more-or-less petty rulers of South Asia the advent of a new native house, and to receive their tribute. Over the next hundred years the Chinese established themselves as the dominant naval power in the Indian Ocean.

In 1369, the very year following his accession, the first Ming Emperor T'ai-tsu sent a mission to the Coromandel Coast of India to announce that event, and another in 1370. When the Yung-lo Emperor came to the Throne in 1402 another expedition went off to Coromandel. Two others followed in 1403, in which year we learn that "ambassadors" from Calicut (*Ku-li*) and Chola (*So-li*) arrived

From William Willetts, "The Maritime Adventures of Grand Eunuch Ho," in Colin Jack-Hinton, ed., *Papers on Early South-east Asian History* (Singapore: The Journal of Southeast Asian History, 1964), pp. 25-6. Reprinted by permission of the publisher. Footnotes omitted.

at the Chinese Court and presented tribute horses to the Emperor, whereupon they were allowed to land their cargo of pepper duty-free. They were presumably only traders.

The frequency and scale of Chinese probes into the Western Ocean now suddenly and dramatically increased, making it appear, as J. V. Mills has said, as though China were attempting a sort of "thalassocracy" * and to turn the Indian Ocean into a Chinese lake for purposes of trade and diplomacy. The man chosen to direct the operation was one Cheng Ho, a Muslim and a eunuch. He had helped the Yung-lo Emperor onto the Throne against the opposition of his nephew, the actual second Ming Emperor Yun-wen (reigned 1398-1402), and had won the reputation of a great diplomat and military strategist. We may wonder, perhaps, at the unusual metamorphosis of a eunuch into a fighter, but we have to believe it in Ho's case, for we are told he had "a stride like a tiger's, and a voice clear and vibrant." His father and grandfather had both been *haj* pilgrims; presumably the tales they had to tell opened up Asian horizons in Ho's mind, and awoke in him a strong desire to see the world.

With Ho in command, a staggering sequence of seven inter-oceanic expeditions now took place.

The Great Stone at Fukien

Some years ago in the yamen at Ch'ang-lo, in the province of Fukien [in China], a stone inscription was discovered, that had been transported thither at some earlier date from the temple of the T'ien Fei, "Celestial Spouse," at that same place. The official who discovered the stone, a certain Mr. Wang Po-ch'iu, wrote a statement of his find in January, 1937. The stone was erected by Cheng Ho and his companions "on a lucky day in the second winter moon of the cyclical year *hsin-hai,* the sixth year of Hsuan-te" (i.e., 5th December, 1431–2nd January, 1432), that is, just before the seventh or last expedition weighed anchor. . . .

[The stone read, in part:]

> The Imperial Ming Dynasty, in unifying seas and continents, sur-passing the three dynasties even goes beyond the Han and T'ang Dynasties. The countries beyond the horizon and at the ends of the

* Dominion over the sea: cf. "thalassocracy of Minos," for the ancient Cretan power-realm in the Mediterranean—ED.

From J. J. L. Duyvendak, *China's Discovery of Africa* (London: Arthur Probsthain, 1949), pp. 28-30. Reprinted by permission of the publisher. Foot-notes omitted.

earth have all become subjects and to the most western of the western or the most northern of the northern countries, however far they may be, the distances and the routes may be calculated. Thus the barbarians from beyond the seas, though their countries are truly distant, with double translation have come to audience bearing precious objects and presents.

The Emperor, approving of their loyalty and sincerity, has ordered us [Cheng Ho] and others at the head of several tens of thousands of officers and flagtroops to ascend more than a hundred large ships to go and confer presents on them in order to make manifest the transforming power of the (imperial) virtue and to treat distant people with kindness. From the third year of Yung-lo [1405] till now we have several times received the commission of ambassadors to the countries of the Western Ocean. The barbarian countries which we have visited are: by way of Chan-ch'eng [Champa], Chao-wa [Java], San-fo-ch'i [Palembang] and Hsien-lo [Siam], crossing straight over to Hsi-lan-shan [Ceylon] in South India, Ku-li [Calicut] and K'o-chih [Cochin], we have gone to the western regions Hu-lo-mo-ssu [Hormuz], A-tan [Aden], Mu-ku-tu-shu [Mogadishu, in Africa], all together more than thirty countries large and small. We have traversed more than one hundred thousand li of immense waterspaces and have beheld in the ocean huge waves like mountains rising sky-high, and we have set eyes on barbarian regions far away hidden in a blue transparency of light vapors, while our sails, loftily unfurled like clouds, day and night continued their course [rapid like that] of a star, traversing those savage waves as if we were treading a public thoroughfare. Truly this was due to the majesty and the good fortune of the Court and moreover we owe it to the protecting virtue of the Celestial Spouse.

* * *

At the end of the inscriptions the different expeditions are carefully enumerated. From them we learn that the first expedition (1405-07) visited Champa, Java, Samudra, Lambri, Ceylon, and Calicut. The second and the third (1407-09 and 1409-11) visited several of the same places and some others in Indonesia and on the coast of India; at Ceylon, during the third voyage, there were difficulties with the king, who was taken to China as a prisoner. The fourth voyage went not only to the previous places but also all the way to Hormuz, while a branch expedition sailed to Bengal (1413-15). It is on this expedition that Mohammedan interpreters such as Ma Huan were taken along. The fifth voyage (1417-19) went even farther, for not only are most of the earlier places visited as well as Hormuz, but also Aden and even Melinda, on the African coast. The avowed object of this expedition was the escorting home of foreign envoys of whom a great many had arrived as a result of the previous expeditions. The sixth voyage (1421-22), undertaken for the same reason, extended as far as Brawa and Mogadisho on the African coast. Finally, the last expedition 1431-33) went to Hormuz.

3 / THE SOPHISTICATION OF ASIAN TECHNOLOGY

Along with the question of whether Asians might have moved west as ably as Europeans moved east (if technology were all), there is the question of whether Asians could have held their own against Europeans in Asia. The following selection suggests that, at least initially, they could.

In 1498 the Portuguese ships under the command of Vasco da Gama, after having sailed around the southern point of Africa, lay off Melinde, on the eastern coast, and the ruler of the port town gave them two of his pilots to go on the crossing to Calicut on the western coast of India. When on board, Da Gama showed his nautical instruments, including wood-and-metal astrolabes, to one of the guides, a Moslem from the northwest Indian coastal region of Gujarat. The "Moor" did not show a single sign of astonishment: the use of such nautical aids was also known to shipping on those routes.

In 1511, when D'Albuquerque attacked the Malay port town of Malacca, the artillery battle carried on by the two sides showed that the Indonesian city was just as well acquainted with the use of big guns as the European seafarers. With the fall of the stronghold three thousand pieces of artillery, including two thousand bronze cannon, most of them of small calibre, fell into the hands of the conquerors. And in the same year Malays also went along to tend the guns on D'Abreu's Portuguese ships in the first voyage further east toward the Moluccas.

In the struggle between the state of Achin and the Portuguese of Malacca in 1564, the Ottomans, the masters of Egypt and the ports on the Red Sea, sent the sultan auxiliary troops, skilled artillery men, and a large quantity of guns and ammunition. In one of the later sieges of Portuguese Malacca by Johore, the ruler of

From J. C. van Leur, "The World of Southeast Asia: 1500-1650," in *Indonesian Trade and Society: Essays in Asian Social and Economic History* (The Hague: W. van Hoeve, Ltd., 1955), pp. 159-60. Reprinted by permission of the publisher. Footnotes omitted.

Achin according to the account of Jan Huyghen van Linschoten sent to the ruler of Johore:

> a peece of Ordinance, such as for greatnes length and workmanship, the like is hardly to bee found in all Christendome (or so well wrought) . . . which I have purposely set down to let you know that they have other kindes of Mettals, and know howe to handle them.

Legaspi, coming to the Philippine—thus, Indonesian—island Cebu in the first Spanish voyage across the Pacific, found there in 1565 a Moslem trader, factor of the sultan of Brunei in North Borneo, and on Luzon and off Mindoro Moslem, Chinese, and Japanese merchants and ships (1565, 1570-72). With the attack made by the Spaniards on Manila in 1570, the place was burned; one thing that went up in flames was a house where artillery was cast, and in which twelve pieces were still to be found.

After they had sailed around the Cape and crossed the Pacific, then, the Portuguese and Spaniards encountered nautical and military techniques which were on an equal footing with European.

4 / EUROPE'S TECHNICAL SUPERIORITY:
THE APPLICATION OF SCIENCE TO TECHNOLOGY

And yet, in spite of such asseverations, there is reason to ascribe to the Portuguese, and certainly to the Europeans who followed them, a certain technical advantage over the contemporary Asians. The following group of extracts indicates this.

Shipbuilding

. . . The rapid initial success of the Portuguese was to no small extent determined by their technical superiority, and that superiority had a scientific foundation. Certainly in some parts of Asia the level of scientific knowledge was no lower than in Europe—after all, Western knowledge of mathematics was mainly Arabic in origin—but in Asia, unlike Europe, there was no connection at all between science and technics, which meant that scientific results were not tested by experimental technology. It was precisely this

From M. A. P. Meilink-Roelofsz, *Asian Trade and European Influence in the Indonesian Archipelago Between 1500 and About 1630* (The Hague: Martinus Nijhoff, 1962), pp. 9, 61. Reprinted by permission of the publisher. Footnotes omitted.

which gave the Portuguese on their first appearance in Asia an advantage which should not be underestimated.

. . .

. . . But the Indians, like the Arabs, must have had a vast and empirical fund of nautical information at their disposal and, armed with this, ships sailed from the west coast of India in northwest, west, and southeasterly directions. The Gujarati ports in particular boasted an extensive fleet of merchant shipping. Like all Arab, Persian, and Indian craft, the Gujarati ships were designed to meet the requirements of the Indian Ocean and its monsoon winds. They were vessels which ran well before the wind, fast freighters with large cargo holds, but capable, too, of maneuvering against the wind. During their construction no rivets were used, instead the planks were lashed together with rope made from coconut fiber, a more suitable material for fastenings than iron, which would rust in the damp of the tropics. Although such a method of fastening planks together need not detract from the sturdiness of construction, these ships could not, in fact, stand up to heavy storms. They were especially exposed to the risk of storms if they did not reach port before the monsoon started blowing. Marco Polo's condemnation of the ships of Hormuz is a case in point: rather than entrust themselves to these vessels, he and his fellow-voyagers chose to follow the long and dangerous overland route to Cathay. A great number of reports dating from later times have also been preserved about the many disasters suffered by these "Moorish" ships. Perhaps this is one reason why the Indians later tried to persuade the Europeans to allow Indian goods to be carried in European ships.

Navigation and Shipbuilding

Charts

If it was the crusading spirit, in the person of Prince Henry, which set the Portuguese upon a career of overseas expansion, crusading zeal was not, of course, the whole story. Courage, discipline,

From J. H. Parry, *The Establishment of the European Hegemony, 1415-1715: Trade and Exploration in the Age of the Renaissance* (New York: Harper & Row, Publishers, Inc. [Harper Torchbooks], 1961), pp. 13-14, 18-19, 21. Originally published as *Europe and a Wider World* (London: Hutchinson & Company Ltd. [Hutchinson University Library], 1949). Reprinted by permission of the publishers.

and organizing ability played their part; and besides these moral considerations must be set another group of factors, commercial and above all technical, which contributed to the astonishing achievements of the Portuguese in two continents in the course of a single century. As an introduction to the narrative of Portuguese exploits, some account must be made of these factors; of the tools available in the fifteenth century for making Prince Henry's dreams a reality.

One of the most obvious characteristics of European civilization is its preoccupation with technical problems and its mastery of a wide range of mechanical devices. Technical skill and the ability to turn theoretical knowledge to practical material ends have been major factors in the extension of European influence round the world, and have forcibly, though not always favorably, impressed all the peoples with whom Europeans have come into contact. This characteristic has been most marked in the last century or century-and-a-half; but it has been an important element in the whole history of European expansion. The scientific knowledge of the time, whether the result of genuine discovery or of the revival of classical knowledge, was turned very quickly to practical account.

In the story of exploration and overseas expansion, three branches of technical development proved to be of the first importance. One was the study of geography and astronomy and its application to the problems of practical navigation. The second was shipbuilding and the development of skill in handling ships. The third was the development of firearms and in particular of naval gunnery. In the first two, at least, of these branches of skill the people of Western Europe drew upon the knowledge either of their classical predecessors or of their eastern neighbors, but applied that knowledge in ways undreamed of by its original discoverers.

.   .   .

. . . At the beginning of the fifteenth century the navigator had no means of finding his position once he lost sight of land, and consequently he took care as a rule not to lose sight of land. At the end of the century, an intelligent and literate navigator had at his disposal several methods of discovering his latitude; he had an agreed estimate of the geographical length of a degree of latitude —eighteen Portuguese leagues, an error of only four per cent; and he had charts on which his observations could be plotted. He had no means of finding his longitude—that was a more difficult problem, not satisfactorily solved until the eighteenth century; but by a combination of observed latitude and dead-reckoning he could keep track of his position tolerably well. Much of the medieval navigator's horror of the open sea had thus been dissipated. All this achievement was due to an unprecedented combination of sea experience and academic knowledge; and the methods really worked. In Vasco da Gama's great voyage to India, which closed the century, there was no more dramatic feature than the accuracy of his navigation and of his first landfall on the South African coast.

Ships

At the beginning of the fifteenth century the seaborne trade of Europe was carried in ships markedly inferior in design and workmanship to the vessels used in many parts of the East; but at the end of the sixteenth century the best European ships were the best in the world. They were, perhaps, less handy and less weatherly than the junks of the China seas, but in general, in their combination of sea-worthiness, endurance, carrying capacity, and fighting power they proved superior to anything else afloat, and they have retained that superiority ever since. The importance of this factor in the story of European expansion is obvious. As in their navigation, so in the design of their ships, European seafarers first borrowed and imitated, then developed and improved their borrowings beyond recognition.

Armament and Shipbuilding

In the descriptions of European expansion the references to European superiority in armament are generally given in static terms. The fact is, however, that after the first wave of expansion in the fifteenth century the European potential in armament production increased dramatically from a quantitative as well as from a qualitative point of view. This made any adjustment of the non-European peoples extremely difficult and their defense problematic, especially because the European progress in the manufacture of guns was accompanied by an equally remarkable progress in the construction of men-of-war and by the development of new techniques of naval warfare.

From Carlo M. Cipolla, *Guns and Sails in the Early Phase of European Expansion, 1400-1700* (London: Collins Publishers, 1965; New York: Random House, Inc. [Pantheon Books], 1965, pp. 74-7, 81. © 1965 by Carlo M. Cipolla. Reprinted by permission of the publishers. Footnotes omitted.

. . . Until the middle of the seventeenth century the main short-comings of artillery for land warfare were slow rate of fire and lack of mobility. The limitations in mobility, however, were over-come in naval warfare and this accounts for the early, extensive, and successful adoption of cannon on board European vessels. Guns made in Tournai were aboard the ships that Louis de Male sent to attack Antwerp in 1336. Genoese galleys had on board fire-arms in 1338 and Venetian boats carried bombards in 1380. Guns were possibly aboard Spanish ships in 1359 and 1372 and by 1381 Catalan merchantmen carried artillery.

These developments came to coincide with a complex set of circumstances which I will cite here only briefly: the closer con-tacts between Mediterranean and Northern navigation; the use of compass and the development of open-sea navigation in the At-lantic area; the shortage of labor due to recurrent plagues after the middle of the fourteenth century and the improvement in the standards of living of the masses which made it more difficult to recruit oarsmen for the galleys; the expansion of trade in the course of the fifteenth century. It is difficult—not to say impossible—to assess the relative importance of each one of these circumstances, but there is no doubt that as a whole they exerted a remarkable impact on the development of shipbuilding and especially on the development of the sailboat. By the end of the fifteenth century the sailing ship had developed to such a point that, while its "rig would have appeared utterly strange to a navigator of the earlier age . . . it seems no exaggeration to say that the ship captains of the age of the great geographical discoveries, or even those of a generation before, would have had but little to learn before taking charge of a ship of Nelson's day."

This progress, no matter how substantial, was of course "purely empirical and often fortuitous." It was unequal, unsystematic, full of successful experiments as well as unconsequential trials. Over-simplifying the matter we may say that the main aspects of the progress were: the adoption after 1300 by Mediterranean merchant-men of the square-rig on the main mast and the consequent transi-tion from the one-masted to the three-masted ships; the noticeable increase in tonnage of merchantmen during the fifteenth century; the greater reliance on artillery for attack and defense.

.   .   .

Exchanging oarsmen for sails and warriors for guns meant essentially the exchange of human energy for inanimate power.

By turning whole-heartedly to the gun-carrying sailing ship the Atlantic peoples broke down the bottleneck inherent in the use of human energy and harnessed, to their advantage, far larger quantities of power. It was then that European sails appeared aggressively on the most distant seas.

II / RELIGION

Nevertheless, though superior technology may be one necessary answer to the question of why Asia was overmatched, it is not sufficient: "European sails appeared *aggressively.*" Technique is no final determinant. Cheng Ho's techniques were startlingly effective, up to a point—a point impressively far from home. Why was there a difference in *will* between Asia and Europe, a will to build on perfectly adequate technical beginnings—potentially fit for any challenge, to meet it or pose it—and to push one's presence around the world?

One form of will is the religious. Weber saw religion as very important for the rise of capitalism, and it was doubtless a factor in the European quest. The long struggle to expel the Muslims from the Iberian peninsula was seen there as part of the Crusades—the only lastingly successful part. The Christian conquest of Granada (the last Muslim kingdom in Spain) and the expulsion of the Jews from Spain were pushed through in Columbus' year, 1492. As the next group of extracts shows, the Iberian captains, Spanish and Portuguese, brought a Christian, crusading zeal to meet the Muslims and pagans at the end of the lines of their voyages.

5 / PROSELYTIZING—AND ECONOMICS

Portuguese Crusades Against the Moors

Portugal came into political history as a border fief of the kingdom of Leon in Spain. Spanish claims to dominion were always resisted,

From J. H. Parry, *The Establishment of the European Hegemony, 1415-1715: Trade and Exploration in the Age of the Renaissance* (New York: Harper & Row, Publishers, Inc. [Harper Torchbooks], 1960), pp. 10-12. Originally published as *Europe and a Wider World* (London: Hutchinson & Company Ltd. [Hutchinson University Library], 1949). Reprinted by permission of the publishers.

and when the Portuguese routed the Castilians in 1385 Portugal was ready to be a self-assertive nation. Now, with a growing sense of national purpose, it would press outward to complete the process of routing the Moors, those other erstwhile claimants to dominion in Portugal. In 1147 foreign knights and adventurers had helped the native Portuguese take Lisbon from the Moors, and four military orders had been created to carry on the struggle. These orders became allied with the monarchy and the commercial classes against the feudal nobility and the clergy—a significant development in the process of expansion (see Selections 23 and 24). When Pope Clement V suppressed the Knights Templar in 1312, the Portuguese Templars were reorganized as the "Order of Chivalry of Our Lord Jesus Christ," for the defense of the faith, the discomfiture of the Moors, and the extension of the Portuguese monarchy. Quite appropriately, the most famous Grand Master of this religious—and national—crusading order was Prince Henry (1394-1460), "the Navigator," the patron of expansion.

The Beginning of European Expansion by Sea

War and trade went hand-in-hand in the later Crusades. Portugal possessed a long ocean seaboard, a considerable fishing and seafaring population, and a powerful commercial class largely emancipated from feudal interference. Portuguese shippers were able and eager to graduate from an Atlantic trade in wine, fish, and salt to more widespread and lucrative ventures in slaves, gold, and spices. The first and obvious object of Portuguese military and commercial expansion was Northwest Africa, where a large and prosperous Muslim community was living almost within hailing distance. Operations began with a sea-borne attack on the town and fortress of Ceuta in 1415.

The expedition to Ceuta was a genuine Crusade, though with a limited and temporary object. It was organized by King John I, partly in order to strike a blow against the Moors by sacking one of their principal harbors—the key to the Mediterranean, Azurara called it; partly to give his sons, who were candidates for knighthood, an opportunity to win their spurs in real battle rather than in the artificial fighting of the tournament. The operation was a brilliant success and the fall of Ceuta struck a resounding blow throughout Europe. Its importance lay, not merely in the fact of the capture, but also in the bold decision to hold the place with a Portuguese garrison instead of razing it to the ground. A European state was undertaking, as a State, the defense and the administration of an overseas possession in Muslim territory. Ceuta offered many possibilities: a base for advance into Morocco, or for an attack on Gibraltar, the other great Moorish fortress in the western Mediterranean; the incentive, and probably to some extent the information, needed for the beginning of systematic African exploration and trade. With the capture of Ceuta the crusading movement passed from its medieval to its modern phase; from a war against Islam in the Mediterranean basin to a general struggle to carry the Christian faith and European commerce and arms round the world.

The most outstanding figure in the first stages of Portuguese—and indeed of European—overseas expansion was Prince Henry of Portugal, nicknamed by English historians "the Navigator." Prince Henry served with great distinction at Ceuta, not only at the capture in 1415, but also three years later when he relieved the Portuguese garrison from a Moorish counterattack. He was intimately concerned with the Crusade in both its forms: its older, narrower form of a Mediterranean war against Moor or Turk, and its newer form of a world-wide strategy for the encirclement of Islam, a strategy in which the exploration of the West African coast and the Atlantic islands was only the first move. He is chiefly remembered now as the organizer of African exploration; but for him the African voyages were a new means to an old end. His many-sided character summed up the best of old and new in the changing times in which he lived. He was both recluse and man of affairs; ascetic and generous host; Governor of the knightly Order of Christ, and friend of seamen, merchants, cartographers, instrument makers; a Catholic Christian of deep and orthodox piety, and a patron of much that was new in learning and science. Under such leadership the beginning of European expansion by sea was no sudden break with the past, but the natural outcome of centuries of crusading hope and frustration.

From Africa to Asia

The same peculiar mixture of commercial and religious motives which had led to the Crusades and had marked the endeavors of Marino Sanudo (1306 and later) also strikes one in the Portuguese expansion from the time of Henry the Navigator (died 1460), "the

From B. Schrieke, "The Shifts in Political and Economic Power in the Indonesian Archipelago in the Sixteenth and Seventeenth Century," in *Indonesian Sociological Studies: Selected Writings of B. Schrieke,* Part One (The Hague: W. van Hoeve Ltd, 2nd ed., 1966), pp. 37-41. Reprinted by permission of the publisher. Footnotes omitted.

first conqueror and discoverer of heathendom," on. In the new expansion, however, there was a third element to be detected, that of the lust for adventure and the ambition of the nobility which had not found any means of expression after the Crusades.

It was actually this factor and the religious factor which in the beginning were the driving forces setting the expansion of the Portuguese in motion; the conquest of Ceuta on the north coast of Africa, the important Mohammedan commercial center from which Christian trading ships were threatened with piracy, gave the initial impetus.

> The expedition against Ceuta, in 1415, which heralded the expansion of Portugal overseas, was not a colonial expedition, it was simply a crusade. But it exerted a decisive influence on the foreign policy of Portugal by giving that country a possession separated from its other provinces by a sea arm and by making it the champion of Christendom against the African Moors.
>
> Portugal was forced to create a navy in order to fight the Moors and provide Ceuta with supplies. Till then a continental power, from that moment on it had maritime interests to defend. Henry the Navigator, a man of genius, enlarged the scene of struggle: he directed it towards new routes where rich lands offered themselves for the taking. He added to the chivalric ambitions which were at the source of the struggle the search for commercial benefits.*

Religious zeal, nourished in the tradition of the Crusades and the remembrance of the bitter struggle with the Moors in the Iberian Peninsula, certainly continued to be an essential motivation. The countless emigrants from the Italian commercial republics who had made their way to Spain and Portugal fanned the desire for enterprise after the capture of Ceuta.

The religious element remained a factor of significance in Spanish politics in later times as well. For the inhabitant of the peninsula a Mohammedan was a "Moor," an object of abhorrence. "It is worthy of comment," as one Arab author of the time writes, "that the Franks only harbor antipathy and hatred for the Mohammedans and their faith; they do not display any aversion for the heathens." Mohammed was for them the devil incarnate. Whoever spared one of his followers failed in his duty, a duty which in most cases was all the more zealously fulfilled because political and commercial interests were benefitted by it.

Thus in 1500 one sees Cabral being commissioned to inform the ruler of Calicut of the hostility the Portuguese had "from ancient days" had toward the Mohammedans, whom they were required to rob of their ships and goods as much as possible in order to please the Lord their God. According to Barros, Cabral was instructed first to urge the Moors and heathens to be converted—for which purpose priests were taken along—but in case they refused to accept the Gospel and at the same time forbade trade, he was to pursue them with fire and sword, and war on them without mercy. As it is put in the letter sent along to the ruler of Calicut from King Manoel:

> ... we may believe that the Lord our God has not ordained such a wondrous matter as our voyage to the Indies merely for the advancement of worldly relations, but also for spiritual profit and the salvation of souls, the which we must value more highly.

And how much religious zeal inspired someone like D'Albuquerque appears from the plans he left unaccomplished at his death: first, to divert the Nile so that Egypt, the heart of Mohammedan opposition, would become waste and void, and, second, after capturing Aden, to attack Mecca from there and destroy it forever. In this way the Crusade ideal continued its influence. For a long time the Portuguese had in mind closing an alliance with the legendary Christian ruler Prester John, whose empire was thought to lie in India; with his help they hoped to be able to bring the crusade against the Moors to a successful end in the heart of their own territory.

Two irreconcilable, envious powers, medieval Christendom and Islam, stood thus face to face, one just as exclusive in its attitude as the other. On the one hand a conglomeration of people of one faith who for ages had been in possession of an extensive and profitable trade which had been constantly increasing for the last three centuries and whose interests entailed the exclusion of other competitors; on the other hand a nation which considered it its "true heritage," "a privilege allowed them through an extraordinary blessing of God," to exterminate the mortal enemies of the faith. Consequently, as soon as the Portuguese began to compete for the monopoly of trade and attempt to drive rivals out of it, among other ways by means of treaties with native rulers, the clash could not be avoided. The seizure and burning of Mohammedan ships by the Portuguese reduced imports to Egypt, while the Portuguese themselves furthermore brought the goods on the European market via the Cape, thus not only avoiding the heavy Egyptian tolls, but at the same time breaking the Egyptian monopoly. The rulers of Gujarat and Aden turned to the sultan of Egypt, who via the famous Fra Mauro, prior of the monastery of Zion on Mount Sinai, sent a remonstrance to the pope in which he threatened to destroy the holy places and wreak vengeance on all Christians if the king of Spain did not stop forcing the Moors to accept Christianity and the king of Portugal did not abandon the voyages to the Indies. The threat was not carried out, but in 1506 and later there were fleets fitted out and pan-Islamic agitation and coalitions the ramifications of which extended as far as the Indonesian archipelago were organized from Egypt, first by the Egyptian Mameluke sultans and later by the Turks, with the aim of ousting the trade of the Portuguese and driving them out of the area they had acquired not long before. Because of a lack of shipbuilding material, such attempts never had much effect, though the struggle was bitter. The Portuguese ships, at the outset most of them built in the Netherlands, were at that time superior both in type and armament, so that however precarious their position sometimes may have been, they were able to brave such attacks. And if their common interests made the Mohammedan nations join together and for a time overlook their quarrels with each other—Turkish conquerors versus Arabs; Malabar, the leading Indian stapling point in the previous period of trade, when the route to the West went via the Persian Gulf instead of the Red Sea, contra Cambay, its newly emerging competitor—such alliances could not be lasting, for the antitheses were only all too real, especially when the Turks attempted to exert their authority also in northern India. Nevertheless there periodically recurred a pan-Islamic expression of resistance to the dominant position held by the Portuguese, so that even Achin and Java contributed their share in it.

Such a state of affairs necessarily led to the establishment of key points for Portuguese trade in the East. After all, the lines of communication with the bases in the mother country were much longer for them than for the Chinese and Indians, who found compatriots or agents everywhere. Furthermore, the latter had not yet had to brave the competition which then began to develop: up to that time the sale of wares via Alexandria had been a certainty, while now the Portuguese were supplying the European market by their own direct importation. Thus they found the Portuguese in their way both as buyers and as sellers. As a matter of fact, the Javanese, too, had felt the need for key points for their trade. . . . For the Portuguese, whose base lay so far away, the need was still greater, partly to assure them of the possibility of sanctions for obtaining the proper fulfilment of contracts. Later the Dutch also found themselves obliged to establish a "rendezvous," discovering that the situation could change after their absence for one or more years and that only by means of such a key point could they keep in regular contact with the rulers with whom they had treaties.

In the case of the Portuguese, there was besides that the fact that the two trade competitors, they and the "Moors," looked upon each other as mortal enemies attempting to do as much damage to each other as possible, and for them it was quite definitely a question of maintaining a monopoly which would put them in a position to set the prices on the market themselves as Egypt and the Italians before them had done. The contracts the fulfilment of which they sought to assure by means of their key points were not only of a political sort, but also economic. In order to make certain the delivery of commercial crops they, like the traders, were accustomed to giving advances and to making gifts or loans to authorities. As more competition arose the risk of losing the money thus invested became greater. The later history of the Dutch Company offers examples on every page of writing off such bad entries. That circumstance also gave rise to a greater need to be able to enforce the fulfilment of contracts the more the willingness to close what were in actuality impracticable agreements was stimulated by the introduction of attractive conditions, for the competition brought with it influence on the parties involved to break delivery contracts with a rival. The Dutch Company, too, was later to take part in such a policy of undermining, just as it was also to taste the bitter fruits of it. As exploitation costs rose higher and higher as the result of such mutual competition, the need to make trade safe, the desire to be able to impose the will of one's own group, in short to establish the rule of that group partly in order thus to bring down general costs, were bound to increase.

Spanish "Missionaries" in the Philippines

The first Spanish contact with the Philippine Islands was in 1521, when Magellan, a Portuguese in the Spanish service, landed there and was killed in the course of the first voyage around the world (1519-22), which he had organized and led until his death. He had accomplished Columbus' purpose, the opening up of a new sea route to the Far East by a voyage westward. From Cortés on, Spanish authorities in Mexico were eager to develop the trans-Pacific route.

When Spain was forced to yield the more highly prized Moluccas to Portugal, the Philippines became a definite goal of Spanish expansion. In 1564 Legaspi sailed with five ships from Navidad in Mexico, under orders to take possession of the Philippines, make converts, make a survey of native products, and establish a return route across the Pacific. The Spaniards occupied Cebu in 1565, and in 1571 they seized Manila.

Two Letters from Miguel Lopez de Legaspi to Philip II

(1)

. . . If this land [the Philippines] is to be settled, to pacify and place it under your royal dominion, in order to civilize its inhabitants and bring them to the knowledge of our holy Catholic faith, for it cannot be sustained by way of trade, both because our articles of barter have no value among them, and because it would be more expense than profit—in order to possess it for pacification, it is most necessary and important that your Majesty maintain here a half-dozen galleys, with which to explore all this archipelago, and make further discoveries. Likewise they could coast along China and the mainland, and find out what there is there, and achieve other things of great importance. The galleys could be built here at very slight cost, because there is plenty of wood and timber. Your Majesty would have only to provide tackle, sails, anchors, and the heavy bolts and nails for these vessels. You would also have to send from Nueva España two skilled shipbuilders, two forges, and two dozen Negroes from those that your Majesty maintains at the harbor at Vera Cruz who might be taken without causing any shortage. Pitch, oakum, and grease, which are not to be had here, could be made without any further cost. The ships could be manned by slaves bought from these natives, or taken from those places which do not consent to obey your Majesty.

Likewise if the land is to be settled, the mines here ought to be worked and fitted up. Since at first it will be difficult and costly

From *The Colonization and Conquest of the Philippines by Spain: Some Contemporary Source Documents, 1559-1577* (Manila: Filipiniana Book Guild, 1965), pp. 127-128, 146-48, 152, 278-79. Reprinted by permission of the publisher. Footnotes omitted.

and very laborious, for many causes and reasons, your Majesty ought to do us the favor of giving up your royal rights and fifths, or a part of them, and for a time suitable, to those working the mines, so that they might reconcile themselves to undertaking it and expending their possessions therein: your Majesty ought likewise to give them permission to buy the slaves, whom these natives barter and sell among themselves, and whom they can use on their estates and for their advantage, without taking them from their land and native home. In everything your Majesty will examine and provide according to your pleasure. May our Lord keep your sacred royal Catholic Majesty, and increase your kingdoms and seigniories for many and prosperous years, as your royal heart desires. From this island of Cubu, June 26, 1568. Your sacred royal Catholic majesty's faithful and humble servant who kisses your royal feet.

(2) Relation of the Filipinas Islands and the Character and Conditions of Their Inhabitants

. . . At present cinnamon is the only article in the land from which we can derive profit; for, as I have said above, the gold supply will always be small until the mines are worked. I believe that if the land is settled and peopled by Spaniards, we shall be able to get plenty of gold, pearls, and other valuable articles. We shall also gain the commerce with China, whence come silks, porcelains, benzoin, musk, and other articles. Thus partly through commerce and partly through the articles of commerce, the settlers will increase the wealth of the land in a short time. In order to attain this, the first and foremost thing to be attempted is colonization and settlement. Through war and conquest, carried on by soldiers, who have no intention to settle or remain in this country, little or no profit will result; for the soldiers will rather impoverish the land than derive profit from it.

If your Majesty looks forward to this land for greater and richer things, it is necessary to people it, and to have a port here; for this land has many neighbors and is almost surrounded by the Japanese islands, China, Xava, Borney, the Malucos, and Nueva Guinea. Any one of these lands can be reached in a short time. This country is salubrious and has a good climate. It is well-provisioned, and has good ports, where can be found abundance of timber, planking, and other articles necessary for building of ships. By sending her workmen, sails, and certain articles which are not to be found here, ships could be built at little cost. Moreover, there is great need of a good port here, for it is very dangerous for large ships to sail very far in among these islands, on account of the shoals and tides hereabout. For this reason, it would be better to build galleys and light boats with oars, to go to the lands above-named, whence they would bring the cargoes for the heavy vessels. Thus the latter would not leave any port of these islands which might be founded for this purpose; and by this method the voyages and trading would be effected with great rapidity in every direction. The large ships would simply come to such ports as I have said, load their cargoes, and return.

I believe that these natives could be easily subdued by good treatment and the display of kindness; for they have no leaders, and are so divided among themselves and have so little dealing with one another—never assembling to gain strength, or rendering obedience one to another. If some of them refuse at first to make peace with us, afterward, on seeing how well we treat those who have already accepted our friendship, they are induced to do the same. But if we undertake to subdue them by force of arms, and make war on them, they will perish, and we shall lose both friends and foes; for they readily abandon their houses and towns for other places, or precipitately disperse among the mountains and uplands, and neglect to plant their fields. Consequently, they die from hunger and other misfortunes. One can see a proof of this in the length of time which it takes them to settle down again in a town which has been plundered, even if no one of them has been killed or captured. I believe that by peaceful and kindly means, they will be easily won over, although it may take some time to do so—because, in all towns where Spaniards have brought peace and not destruction, the natives have always begged for friendship, and have offered to pay tribute from what they gather and owe in their lands. And although at times they do not fulfill their promise, it is not to be wondered at; for the country is not yet sufficiently settled and secure. I am sure that, when this is so, they will be subdued and will do whatever is justly commanded them.

These natives will be easily converted to our holy Catholic faith, for most of them are heathens, excepting the natives of Borney and Lucon (who are chiefly Moros), and a few converted chiefs of these islands. These Moros have little knowledge of the law which they profess, beyond practicing circumcision and refraining from pork. The heathens have no law at all. They have neither temples nor idols, nor do they offer any sacrifices. They easily believe what is told and presented forcibly to them. They hold some superstitions, such as the casting of lots before doing anything, and other wretched practices—all of which will be easily eradicated, if we have some priests who know their language, and will preach to them. Certainly, there is a great opportunity to serve God, our Lord, and to expand and extol our holy Catholic faith, if our sins do not hinder the work. . . .

Letter from Martin de Rada
to the Marquis de Falces

. . . If his Majesty wishes to get hold of China, which we know to be a land that is very large and rich and of high civilization, with cities, forts, and walls much greater than those of Europa, he must first have a settlement in these islands [the Philippines]; first, because we cannot pass safely among the so many islands and shoals that lie along the coast of China with ships of high freeboard, but must use oared vessels; secondly, also, because in order to conquer a country so large and that has so vast a population, one must have aid and refuge near at hand, for any contingency that might arise. However, as I have been informed both by Portuguese and by Indians who trade with the Chinese, as well as by a Chinese who was captured a while ago in a junk, the people of China are not at all warlike. They rely entirely on numbers and on the fortification of their walls. It would decapitate them, if any of their forts were taken. Consequently, I believe (God helping), that they can be subdued easily and with few forces.

I have wished to write this, for I trust in our Lord that this land may, through the medium of your Excellency, receive the faith, and that we shall have an entrance into China; but, on account of our great uncertainty and because we do not know whether his Majesty will order us to abandon this land, we have not dared to baptize. I believe that if we had put our hands to baptism, we would already have more than twenty thousand Christians. As soon as we know the king's will they will all accept our faith easily.

May our Lord, etc.
Cebú, July eight, 1569.

Letter from Guido de Lavezaris
to Philip II

. . . Inasmuch as this island of Lucon [i.e., Luzon] is so large, and as, for the preservation of the natives, we need some settlements of Spaniards to protect and defend them, and teach them our holy Catholic faith, it seemed best to send Captain Juan de Salcedo with seventy or eighty soldiers to people the coast of Los Ylocos, on the shores of a river called Bigan. There I ordered him to found the town of Fernandina in memory of the prince, our master (may he live many happy years); and I continued to apportion, in the name of your Majesty, all that had been discovered and won over thereabout, reserving for your Majesty what had been ordered me through your royal decree.

The Chinese, in view of the kind treatment that they have always received and do receive at our hands, continue to increase their commerce each year, and supply us with many articles as sugar, wheat, and barley flour, nuts, raisins, pears, and oranges; silks, choice porcelain and iron; and other small things which we lacked in this land before their arrival. This year they gave a drawing of the coast of China, made by themselves, which I am sending to your Majesty.

There is great need in these regions of Franciscan, Dominican, and Theatin religious, and of some ecclesiastics, for the conversion of the natives. The Theatins are much and especially needed; for, as an eyewitness, I know the great results that they have obtained in Yndia. With the coming of more people, it will be necessary to found a few Spanish settlements in this island of Lucon, which is large, and in other islands; for already these natives are being baptized daily, and are embracing our holy faith and religion. They are very quiet and reconciled, and will be more so when many religious of the said orders have arrived; for at present we have only ten Augustinian religious here, and they are not sufficient for the great labor demanded of them. I repeat that the service of your Majesty requires the presence here of Franciscan religious and of some Theatins. . . .

6 / THE CLASH OF RELIGIONS
AND THE DAWN OF UNDERSTANDING: MEXICO

So far in this section on religion, the reader will have noticed some extraneous matter—a certain concern with purposes other than religious. We shall come back to this. In the meantime, lest we come to think that religion is only a cover, not a serious issue in the problem of expansion, let us consider some men who took it utterly

From J. H. Elliott, "Chronicles of the Conquest," *The New York Review of Books*, II, No. 6 (April 30, 1964), 12-13. © 1964 by The New York Review. Reprinted by permission of *The New York Review of Books* and the author.

seriously. They show us some of the implications of religion for expansion, and of expansion for religion.

The Spanish conquest of Mexico, consummated in the sixteenth century, was of incalculable importance in spreading the idea of religious assimilation of the outside world to Europe.

It is, above all, [the] impression of immediacy which gives the Conquistadors' accounts of the Mexican campaigns their freshness and readability, One senses the comradeship in arms—"there was no rioting or quarrelling, but on the contrary, everything was shared equally, and whatever belonged to one belonged to the others." This close-knit little band of Conquistadors was moving through a strange and alien world, surrounded by a population that appeared treacherous, guileful, and appallingly barbarous. Overshadowing every account is the sense of almost stunned horror at the idolatry and cannibalism of the natives. Even Francisco de Aguilar, who said he had delved into the history of Greece, Rome, and Persia, and had read about the rites performed in Portuguese India, considered that in none of these countries were there "such abominable forms of worship as they offered to the Devil in this land."

The great gulf that separated the religion of the conquerors from that of the conquered made it terribly difficult for the Spaniards to understand the New World that they were now attempting to incorporate into the Old. But in the greatest of them, Hernán Cortés, the horror of idolatry did not prevent a genuine appreciation of the constructive achievements of the Aztecs, and a high hope that, once their idols were cast down, they would be ready to take their place as worthy citizens of the empire of Charles V. Cortés's third letter, dominated as it is by the gruelling story of the siege and conquest of Tenochtitlán, inevitably reflects less sympathy for certain aspects of the Indian character and achievement than his first two letters do, but it does, on the other hand, bring out very clearly his increasing admiration for the Indians as fighters. Cortés conveys memorably the heroism of Aztec resistance during the final days of the siege, and it was precisely the valor and the heroism of the vanquished which were to provide Cortés's secretary and chaplain, Lopez de Gomara, with the ideal background for the great history of the Conquest that he published in 1552.

. . . Gomara, like Bernal Díaz, has his limitations. The classical models are too close, and Mexico too far away. The New World, remote and incomprehensible, is little more than a spectacular, if carefully painted, backcloth against which the deeds of his hero are enacted. He is capable of pity for the Indians, just as he is also capable of an occasional devastating irony at the expense of the greed and folly of the Conquistadors. He is ready to express admiration for the Aztecs' skill in craftsmanship and construction— an admiration no doubt fostered by his conversations with Cortés, although one is left with an uneasy feeling that he is at the same time exploiting the achievements of the Indians in order to heighten the drama and to dispel any impression that Cortés was expending his military genius in a series of skirmishes against a bunch of savages. But the Indians remained for him, as for the majority of the Conquistadors, a barbarous race, "by nature frivolous and turbulent," given to the most bestial practices, and notoriously prone to consort with the devil.

Was the gulf between Christian Spaniard and heathen Indian so wide, then, as to be insurpassable? Gomara, like most of his countrymen, lacked even the desire to understand. The very identification of the Indians with the devil and all his works made the mental effort of comprehension too great for a people that was consciously dedicating its energies to a relentless war on the Antichrist. And was not this spiritual warfare itself the supreme, and perhaps the only, justification of the Conquest? Religion, therefore, appeared to bar the way against any attempt by the conquerors to see the world, however dimly, through the eyes of the conquered.

Yet paradoxically it was, in the long run, to be the very differences in religion which brought the first glimmers of understanding. How this came about is shown in a remarkable work, *The History of the Indies of New Spain,* by Fra Diego Durán. . . . He had come to New Spain as a child, and entered the Dominican Order in Mexico City in 1556. As a missionary, and especially as one who had been brought up in close contact with the Indians and spoke their language perfectly, he was uniquely placed to understand them, assuming he wished to do so. It was precisely his religion which, instead of inhibiting the attempt at comprehension, provided the vital stimulus. "I have been moved," he explains, "to undertake this task and to recount the ancient idolatries and false religion . . . by realizing that those of us who are concerned in teaching the Indians will never fully succeed in getting them to know the true God unless the superstitious ceremonies and worship of false gods can first be obliterated from their memories." But this could never be achieved unless the missionaries first understood the nature and the magnitude of the problem with which they were faced, and this required a deep knowledge of native history and mythology.

As a result, Durán set out to relate the story of Aztec history as seen through Aztec eyes. His chronicle can not, for this very reason, be taken as a reliable guide to the history of Mexico in the fourteenth and fifteenth centuries. It inevitably lacks perspective, in that it is focused on the Aztecs of Mexico-Tenochtitlán to the virtual exclusion of the various other tribes and kingdoms; and one would imagine from reading it that, in the long and sanguinary list of wars, the Aztecs were invariably the innocent, and victorious, victims of unprovoked aggression. But as an insight into the Aztecs' view of their own past, Durán's chronicle is of inestimable value, and if the reader tires of the long catalogue of deceit, treachery, and bloody battles, he can find relief in Durán's retelling of a number of poignantly beautiful legends.

Durán's work is of great interest for historians of the Conquest not only because it culminates in a description of the Conquistadors through Aztec eyes, but also because of Durán's personal attitude and reactions to the scenes that he describes. In spite of the gruesome stories he relates, his understanding of, and sympathy for, the Indian emerges in his occasional personal asides, and in his unflagging willingness to take the Aztec narrative of events on its own terms. In one passage of the chronicle, not reproduced in this edition, he asks: "In what land on earth have there been so many just and well-devised laws as in this land, and where else have kings been so obeyed and their laws so scrupulously observed?" But he always remains this side of uncritical admiration. He knows his Indians too well to entertain many illusions. All he asks is that they should be seen as they really are, and understood in their own context. If this is done, the comparisons between Indians and Spaniards are not quite so unflattering to the Indians as contemporaries often made them appear.

In Durán, therefore, the apparently unbridgeable gulf is at last beginning to be bridged. The horror of idolatry remains. But the stunned reaction of the Conquistadores, and the uncomprehending irony of Gomara, are here replaced by a dawning comprehension. In the person of Diego Durán, a first generation Mexican, the history of the Conquest becomes for the first time the history not of the conquerors but of the conquered, and a fresh dimension— the dimension of sympathetic understanding—is tentatively added to the process by which the Old World took possession of the New.

7 / RELIGIOUS UNIVERSALISM (1):
EUROPEAN SPIRITUAL APPROPRIATION OF ASIA

*"The process by which the Old World took possession of the New":
here "possession," so often a political word or an economic word,
takes on "a fresh dimension" itself. For ecumenical religion could
certainly be more than a rationalization of political and economic
purposes; it could imply, quite seriously, a widening cultural em-
brace, to take in the world, the veritable world, not just one
"world" or another. In the sixteenth century, as the European empires began to be fashioned and European ("Christian") culture
acquired its first tint, or taint, of a modern imperialistic color,
Christian ("European") culture opened towards a modern cosmopolitanism. Whether other cultures were to be broken, for a
world-wide European hegemony, or whether they were to be as-
similated in a world-wide syncretism, a Christian expansionist impulse had something to do with the shaping of the world.*

*In the following selection, we see how an emphasis on rational-
ism in theology was related to the intellectual problem of assimila-
ting the vast new worlds of the discoveries and explorations. And
the impending conflict of faith and reason (the latter championed
by "the reformers of the Enlightenment," referred to in this selection) was foreshadowed here. The same evidence that, in Guillaume
Postel's mind, pointed to the immanence (rationally discernible) of
Christian truth everywhere could be turned against the Christian
faith; for the faith, after all, was historically linked with a specific
revelation. Christian forms and formulations, then—i.e., the specific trappings of a particular manifestation of Postel's idea of Truth
—might be rejected as just an inessential version of a universal
which would be a foreign version to non-Europeans and therefore
ripe for rejection. The Chinese, for example, with an invincible
feeling for their own history, were not about to let themselves be
annexed to someone else's, even when—especially when—the historically Western offering was supposed to be suprahistorical, the
universal Truth. Instead, as a friendly but unconverted Chinese
remarked to Mateo Ricci (the famous Jesuit who labored in China
around the turn of the seventeenth century), what Jesus was for*

From William J. Bouwsma, *Concordia Mundi: The Career and Thought of
Guillaume Postel (1510-1581)* (Cambridge, Mass.: Harvard University Press,
1957), pp. 208-12, 217-18, 272-73, 296. Reprinted by permission of the publisher.
Footnotes omitted.

Europe, Confucius was for China and Buddha for "the Indies."
Thus, Asian resistance to Christians as Europeans was naturally
not disarmed. Yet, universalism might make Christians see the
world as naturally one, all-Christian.

. . . Universal salvation, not condemnation, was [the] real concern
[of Guillaume Postel (sixteenth-century theologian, humanist, and
Arabist—ED.)]; and his conviction that God worked, even through
pagan beliefs, to save all mankind is constantly reflected in his
treatment of contemporary paganism.

He found evidences of valid religious understanding in every cor-
ner of the world. In part his interest was narrowly practical; he
urged Christian missionaries to exploit the knowledge of Christ to
be found in so many places outside the Christian world. But there
was another element as well in Postel's attitude: a profound conviction of the wide diffusion of religious truth. To assemble illustra-
tions of its dispersion would perhaps justify his own universalism
and modify the parochial dogmatism of the West. He proposed to
demonstrate that Christendom had no monopoly even on the most
important truths of all. For the historicity of the Flood, therefore,
he appealed to the agreement of the whole world: to Christians,
Jews, and Mohammedans, of course, but also to classical antiquity
(in the myth of Pyrrha and Deucalion) and to the peoples of the
Indies. To confirm his belief that the last age would bring unity
to the world, he referred not only to the peoples of the Books, but
also to the Brahmans. He was struck by the promptness with which
the natives of America venerated the Scriptures as the source of
truth; and he discerned obscure prototypes of Christianity among
the Indians of Mexico.

But he was fascinated above all by the religions of the Orient,
together with the civilizations which accompanied them. Postel was
an ardent reader of accounts of Oriental travel, and his reactions
provide an extraordinary example of how knowledge of the outside
world was enlarging the perspectives of the European mind. Much
of his information was no doubt erroneous, and some of it he mis-
understood; but his credulity is a further witness to his enthusiasm.
Eventually he devoted most of a book, his *Merveilles du monde,* to
a demonstration of the superiority of East to West.

This superiority rested ultimately, he believed, on the fact that
the original earthly paradise had been located in the Orient; and
traces of its primitive perfection had never completely disappeared.
For this reason the East was still the richest region of the world.

Its arts and manufactures continued to be the finest: "All things that we hold in the West as of extraordinary artifice are like mere shadows of Oriental excellences." Miraculous plants and animals flourish only in the Orient, among them the wonderful boranetz bush, which bears as its fruit a fully developed lamb; and a marvelous tree which produces at once bread, wine, sugar, oil, silks, linens, all kinds of clothing, fire, and many other useful things. Tutelary geniuses, too, Postel believed, are stronger in the East than elsewhere in the world, and all magical arts flourish there with special efficacy. Even the human being of the East is superior to Western man: "the Oriental understanding is the best in the world." Postel seems almost too ready to admit the inferiority of his own civilization.

But for him the secular perfections of the East, great as they may have been, were overshadowed by its religious virtues, both intellectual and practical. In the remote past, he pointed out, God had recognized the religious power of the Eastern mind by bestowing knowledge of Christ's birth on the three magi. Postel wavered, however, between two explanations for this religious excellence of the East. On the one hand he declared that Jewish revelation had in an early form been carried eastward by the children born to Abraham by his various concubines. Before dispatching them to find new homes in the Orient, their father had given them "divine doctrine with their magic or astrology, of which even till today they retain the odor, along with a very great knowledge of astrology superior to all the world." This view corresponded to his conviction of the Jewish origin of all wisdom. On the other hand Postel insisted also on the rationality of religious truth; and the superiority of human reason in the Orient suggested to him an alternative explanation. Persians, Indians, Chinese, Caucasians, Cathayans, and Japanese alike, he believed, relied on natural reason as the supreme guide to religious truth.

He was most fully informed, through the communications of Francis Xavier, about the religion of Japan; and, on the strength of this information, he envisioned Japan as a kind of utopia of natural reason in which might be discerned both shadowy prototypes of Christian doctrine and practice and anticipations of his own recommendations for the human race. He believed that the Japanese had approached Christianity in many ways. They worshiped an idol with three heads, in obvious recognition of the Trinity; they venerated a virgin mother who interceded on their behalf before God; and they preserved the legend of her son, Xaca, who, said Postel, "is nothing but a vague shadow taken from the

Gospel story." The Japanese were also monotheists; they believed in a future life with rewards and punishments; they practiced a form of monasticism based on life in common; they fasted, prayed, and preached. They also believed firmly in primogeniture, and in just such a leadership of the religious community by the prince as Postel recommended for the West.

We may discern several motives in Postel's praise for the Orient. One, no doubt, was the inherited tendency of the European to look eastward for the sources of his culture; and in Postel this had been reinforced by the conventional interest of the devotee of esoteric thought in the "wisdom of the East." Another, certainly, was to justify his own doctrines. By discerning them in the East, he was able to give to some of them a universal validity. But he was concerned above all with the description of a standard of faith and conduct which the West might use for its own reform. Postel intended the perfections of a non-Christian society to serve as the sharpest of reproaches to an erring Christendom. He was not merely thinking of the Japanese when he wrote that if they would only do in the name of Jesus what they now practiced, they would be "the most perfect men in the world." The moral was for his fellow Europeans: if they would only practice what they now professed in the name of Jesus, *they* would be the most perfect men in the world. Indeed, he could be explicit enough:

> [God] has thus retained the Orient in good works, so that there is no life more perfect, and on the contrary we see in the Occident, where the sovereignty of Evangelical doctrine reigns as much as has been possible until this day, that there is as if nothing remained of the true purity of Christian works or perfections, so that Occidental life is a scandal to all the world, and chiefly among the ecclesiastical princes and judges who ought to respond in Sanctity to their office.

The same impulse which underlay More's *Utopia* thus seems to have impelled Postel to describe the perfections of the Orient. The fact that Japan was somewhere, rather than nowhere, gave to Postel's ideal the advantage of concreteness, but it also generally confined him to the facts. But the facts, unfortunately, were still relatively few; and Postel's description of the ideal state consequently remained incomplete. He could supply enough, however, to reveal a most important function of the *ecclesia generalis*: to shame the *ecclesia specialis* by its virtuous example. The generosity of his conception is startling in a Christian of the sixteenth century; for Postel, it must be remembered, was not offering to his contemporaries either a fantasy (however serious) or an academic idealization of the past. He was praising, to the disadvantage of his own society, a vital aspect of the present. We may well rank him, therefore, although a generation before Montaigne, with the reformers of the Enlightenment, as well as with the men of the Renaissance. In Postel the potentialities of the Erasmian movement come close to full actualization.

· · ·

Both the eschatological significance of world unity and the notion that universal empire would be finally achieved by the French had deep roots in the Middle Ages. The conception of a world empire blessed with ideal peace and order stems both from Jewish messianism and from ancient prophecies of a Golden Age associated with the *Pax Romana*. Christian interpreters, particularly under the influence of Augustine, had conceived its leader, the prince of peace, as a heroic champion against the forces of discord in this world, the heathens, heretics, and rebels; and the Christian sibylline writings which transmitted the whole tradition to the Middle Ages had suggested that at the end of his reign the emperor who had managed to enforce Christian peace upon the world would at last march to Jerusalem and lay down his crown on Golgotha. Then would follow the Last Judgment and the end of the world.

The assignment of the task of leadership to France was also very old. Postel claimed, in fact, extensive support for his views among classical writers, as well as in "the sovereign reasons and authorities of civil and canon law, of the Old and New Testaments and of astrology." Such claims chiefly reveal, no doubt, Postel's remarkable ability to read his own thoughts in any venerable writer; but there was actually much medieval precedent behind him. By the tenth century, legends of Charlemagne had combined with the familiar motifs of Christian eschatology; and Adso of Montiérender had insisted that a last great king of the Franks was still to come who would lay down his scepter and crown upon the holy sepulcher. The tradition of the *Gesta Dei per Francos* added further weight to the notion of a special role for France; and in the thirteenth century Joachimite and anti-Ghibelline notions in Italy converged with a growing interest among French royalists in the imperial title to give additional impetus to the idea. Thus, while the Carmelites of southern Italy were ascribing to the legendary Saint Angelus a prophecy that the French king and the pope would together free the Holy Land from the infidels, and the Italian followers of Joa-

chim were making much of the coincidence that the lily was the
symbol both of France and the last age of the world, Pierre Dubois
was encouraging French hopes of world empire. Lull himself,
though addressing his pleas primarily to the papacy, appealed to
Philip the Fair in a work entitled *De natali parvuli pueri Jesus*;
here the Virgin herself points to the French king as the hope of
Christendom. The Italian prophetic tradition was naturalized in
France by John of Rupescissa (whom Postel cited) in the fourteenth
century; and it was given further currency through the works of
Telesphorus, which were widely circulated. Similar prophecies lay
in the background of the French invasion of Italy in 1494, strength-
ened by the claims of France to the universal empire of the Pale-
ologi; agitators like Jean Michel and Guillauche of Bordeaux
promised to the French king the recovery of the Holy Land and the
universal monarchy. At the very end of the fifteenth century
Lefèvre published a part of Lull's *De natali Jesus*; and the writings
of Telesphorus were printed at Venice in 1515. That such ideas
persisted in Postel's own generation we know, aside from his own
writings, from Rabelais, who facetiously traced the descent of
universal empire from the Assyrians through the Medes, the Persians, the Macedonians, the Romans, and the Greeks, until its final
inheritance by the French, whose position as seventh in the series
suggests the sabbath of world history, the millennium preceding
Judgment Day.

.   .   .

The geographical discoveries, together with the missionary activity
which accompanied them, both stimulated Postel's zeal to finish
the task of evangelization and gave him further cause to believe
that a great new day in the history of the world was at hand. He
had no illusions about the motives of the discoverers; he saw clearly
enough that "avarice, curiosity, the desire for glory, voluptuousness,
and in sum human and sensual pleasure, have been the cause of the
navigation now both in the Atlantic and in Shemic or East India."
But he perceived in this circumstance only further proof of the high
design of Providence, which could so marvelously produce good out
of the evil purposes of men. He attached special importance to the
rediscovery of the Orient, in which he located the original earthly
Paradise, marks of which, he was convinced by the glowing accounts
of travelers, still survived. The expansion of Christianity in the
East signified to him, therefore, the reappropriation by the children
of God of their first Eden, the recovery of primal innocence and

bliss. But the essential fact for Postel was that, "through the navigation of Spain, almost all men have received Christ; and they recognize the Creator of heaven and earth."

.   .   .

Postel's interest in the non-European world may be considered from still another standpoint: he provides important, and fairly early, evidence of the impact of the geographical discoveries, and of the contacts with alien peoples which resulted, on the European mind. Postel's reaction was influenced by the religious conceptions into which he managed to absorb everything that struck his mind, and by his humanist proclivities, a fact itself of some importance in illuminating the process of Europe's intellectual adaptation to her new-found place in a larger world. He began with an insistence on the providential character of the discoveries; he next proceeded to establish a series of religious ties which bound the non-European peoples to Christianity; and he emerged with an attitude of striking receptiveness, at times bordering even on humility, to the accomplishments of the non-European world. Later generations would largely discard the religious apparatus which had helped Postel to this conclusion, but his cosmopolitanism was to remain, at least as an ideal.

8 / RELIGIOUS UNIVERSALISM (2): ASIAN SPIRITUAL WITHDRAWAL

Postel's religious cosmopolitanism made the world seem (as we have suggested) naturally one, all-Christian. This brand of immanent universalism was not itself a direct spur to expansion. But a vision like Postel's, a vision of the world unified by an immanent Truth, implied, nevertheless, that the religious charter for unification originated at home, in the Christian revelation. Accordingly, it also implied that the expansion of Europe, which revealed the immanent ideal oneness to Europe, was a warrant for further expansion, to make the ideal realized, in history.

Now, Europe was not the only home of a universal spirit. The existence of rival universals made the particulars important, and where historical cultures were strongest (e.g., in China, as distinct from the Philippines), Christians, in their spiritual thrust, were generally repelled. But at least they were on the offensive. What

From Sir George B. Sansom, *The Western World and Japan* (London: The Cresset Press, 1950), pp. 49-52, 70. Reprinted by permission of the publisher.

made Confucianism, for example—one of the rivals—so passive in comparison? It had a vision no less ecumenical than the Christian. Yet no one was driven to carry the Confucian version of truth around the world. There must have been something differentiating these types of universalism.

In the spirit of St. Paul, Christian universalism, we have suggested, was supracultural, transhistorical. As a deduction from its premises, it could foster expansion out from lands already Christian to newly discovered lands of potentially Christian souls. Confucian universalism, however, was supremely cultural, rooted in a Chinese culture that was an absolute. It was (high) Culture in the abstract, not just (in the anthropologist's sense) a culture, relative to time and place. Its values were universal, then, like the Christian, but Confucian universalism was a criterion, a standpoint, not a point of departure. It was considered to apply to all the world (all "under-Heaven": T'ien-hsia, both "the Empire" and "the world," where the "Son of Heaven" ruled). And it was open to all. But Confucianists as pragmatists accepted cultural differences as the way of the world, always producing candidates for the title of barbarian. From the point of view of normative Confucianism, wedded to culture and history and antimessianic to the core, the barbarians are always with us. From the point of view of normative Christianity, transcending culture and history (those marks of distinction between "Jews and Greeks"), the pagans are not always with us: let missionaries go overseas, seek them out, convert them. The "Kingdom of God" was nowhere in the world. But the "Middle Kingdom," the point of balanced perfection in the world, under-Heaven, was at home. Whatever it was that sent Chinese into Southeast Asia before the Portuguese ever got there, it had nothing to do with any pretensions to bearing out a Word.

Other Asian world-views, more properly called religious than the culture-bound agnosticism of the Confucian literati, also faced Christianity in Asia. Here, in the next pair of extracts, are some opinions about their relative lack of dynamism.

A Theory of Cyclical Thinking and the Inhibition of Progress

It might be said, in more general terms, that it was the birth in Europe of a doctrine of perfectibility that impelled European states to extend their influence into Asia. As Europeans, under the influence of startling scientific discoveries, came to think that an increase in material benefits could be equated with an advance in human happiness, it was natural that they should look abroad for more wealth and knowledge, since these were the true ingredients of that continuous progress in which they were beginning to believe.

In Asiatic countries no such optimism prevailed as to human destiny. In the great religious and philosophical systems of India the life of mankind is not conceived of as having an end towards which it gradually moves, and certainly man is not seen as the master of his own fate, able to subdue natural forces or at least to turn them to his own ultimate benefit. The flux of existence is thought of not as a progress towards a desirable goal, but as an infinite series, without beginning or end, of cycles of growth and decay. Nothing can be more uncongenial to the European mind than the teaching of Buddhist scriptures (which is not contradicted by Hinduistic beliefs) as to the lack of meaning or purpose in the material universe. Their descriptions of worlds that grow only to perish by flame or flood or stormy violence are such as to induce melancholy in all but the most sanguine and euphoric Occidental.

When a cycle is ended by fire, at first a great world-destroying rain-cloud rises and a great downpour takes place in the hundred thousand myriad world systems. Men bring forth their seeds and sow them, but when the crops begin to grow the rain is completely cut off. Water dries up, and it does not rain for many hundred years, many thousand years, many hundred thousand years. After a long time has passed since the end of the rains, burning suns manifest themselves, one after another. Their heat strikes down uninterruptedly and at length the hundred thousand myriad world systems are a mass of flame. Then after a long time the rains begin again, and presently the sun and the moon and the constellations reappear, and the sequence of day and night, summer and winter, sowing and harvest is resumed. But lust and greed and craving also return, and in due time the aeons of dissolution and quiescence and formation begin again in an eternal repetition of cycles. But there is no progress, no beginning and no end.

Such a view of the fruitlessness of man's endeavor doubtless explains in part why the confidence of European invaders was met by no determined opposition from the peoples of countries under strong Buddhist or Hinduistic influence. At the same time it is significant that as Buddhism moved towards the Far East its pessimism grew thinner, and (as we shall see) Far Eastern peoples, notably the Chinese and the Japanese, proved less acquiescent than Indians in their attitude towards Western intrusion, with its summons to act and to decide.

. . .

. . . Although in ancient times Indian ships had sailed distant seas and had carried Hindu colonists far from their native lands, later Hindu customs, particularly the caste system, were unfavorable to foreign travel. Brahmin orthodoxy, for instance, required (and still nominally requires) a purification (*panipatya*) of every man who has crossed "the black water."

A Theory of Religious Resignation and Immobility

Inventors of machines are not the monopoly of one country or one period, much less of England of the eighteenth century. Millennia before Watt, Hero had designed the steam-engine, but, being an economic superfluity, it remained the plaything of its inventor. Likewise, in India in the sixteenth century at the time of Akbar, a great scientist named Mir Fathullah Shirazi made many remarkable mechanical inventions, which had no bearing whatsoever on the economic conditions of that age. . . .

. . .

. . . Asian trade, industry and technology did not lag behind Europe in the Middle Ages. What is, then, the reason why Asia could not produce an Industrial Revolution and the genius of inventors like Mir Fathullah Shirazi went in vain like flowers blooming in a wilderness? . . .

In Asia about the beginning of the second millennium of the Christian era religion in the sense of orthodoxy, obscurantism, superstition, and dogma seeped into the mentality of the people. Islam, Buddhism, Hinduism, and Christianity (Nestorian), the principal religions of Asia, tended towards a devotional mysticism, on the one hand, and a complex formalism, on the other. They instilled a spirit of rigidity, exclusivism, and resignation and kindled a desire for ethereal, otherwordly, and superhuman objectives. The upsurge of nomadic peoples and their adoption of these religions further intensified their supernatural character. . . .

. . .

. . . Though Asia did not lag behind Europe in industrial,

From Buddha Prakash, *The Modern Approach to History* (Jullundur, Delhi, Ambala: University Publishers, 1963), pp. 289, 299-300, 310-11. Reprinted by permission of the publisher.

commercial, and technological spheres up to about the middle of the eighteenth century, it suffered from social stagnation and decadence as a result of the ascendancy of religious orthodoxy and traditional rigidity. This explains why Asia had nothing like the Industrial Revolution, which changed the techniques of production, or the Scientific Revolution, which enlarged the horizons of the mind, or the French Revolution, which laid the foundations of democracy and the rule of law. It is against this general background that the achievements of a Watt or a Crompton and the failure of a Fathullah Shirazi are to be considered.

9 / RELIGIOUS VERSUS ECONOMIC MOTIVATIONS

The last selection's single-cause religious explanation of Asian placidity, hardly a satisfactory one, must cast some doubt on any similar explanation of European élan. In any case, Islam should not be homogenized with other non-European religions. The early surge of Islam into several continents and oceans make it a poor example of an intrinsically devitalizing religion. Technological and political considerations aside, when the Portuguese came to Asia there was little to choose between Christian and Muslim religious determination.

The following pair of extracts refer to Muslim dedication in the face of the Christian assault. (They refer also, however, to Asian religious rivalries that the Westerners could exploit.)

Two Kinds of Penetration

Rival Conquests: Political and Religious

. . . The spread of Islam in the [East Indies] archipelago began at approximately the same time as the arrival of the Portuguese. Their appearance was in a sense an extension of the Crusades, and furthermore amounted to competition with earlier Asian trade to the West, which was channeled primarily through the Persian Gulf. As soon as the Portuguese arrived in India in 1498 they and the Moslems looked upon each other as their archenemies there. Protests of the Moslem states to the pope were of no avail. By the time the Portuguese influence reached the archipelago

From B. Schrieke, "Ruler and Realm in Early Java," *Indonesian Sociological Studies: Selected Writings of B. Schrieke, Part Two* (The Hague: W. van Hoeve Ltd., 1955), pp. 308-309. Reprinted by permission of the Royal Tropical Institute, Amsterdam, and the publisher. Footnotes omitted.

the Moslems had a head start on them in most places, and succeeded in forming certain centers, of which Achin is the best known on Sumatra and Banten on Java. A similar development can be seen in the Moluccas. The expansion of Islamic power, then, was the result of anti-Christian propaganda. Furthermore Islam, as a consequence of the mystic elements which had infiltrated it, was highly adaptable; the spiritual momentum was provided by the scholars, among whom were the *walis,* or saints, on Java. Ibn Battuta met Persian scholars on Sumatra, and the Dutch Company repeatedly had to take steps against Moslem "popes." The propaganda was further nourished by the mystical *tarikats* and by influences from Mecca. One finds poor members of sherif families in India and Achin, and the Arab sources record a Meccan embassy to the grand mogul which later went on to Achin. The scholars of the Moslem West again and again fostered an orthodox reaction to heretical developments in the faith.

Rival Camps: the Question of Solidarity

In making an assessment of Portuguese activity in Asia, it should be remembered that, as regards both naval strategy and later commercial and political relations between Europe and Asia, it was the Portuguese who laid the foundations of the policies which were later adopted and carried even further by the northern Europeans. In their diplomatic relations with the native rulers and in the conclusion of contracts both Dutch and English followed the example set by the Portuguese. Like the Portuguese, the Dutch concentrated their Asian trade on one stapling center and port of loading. There is remarkably close agreement between the Portuguese records relating to the salary of overseas officials and those of the later Dutch East India Company. The Portuguese even supply more details about employment records. The northern Europeans also adopted the system of passes introduced by the Portuguese on the strength of their claims to mastery of the seas, by which they reserved to themselves the right to confiscate the goods of anyone sailing the seas without their permission. And even though it ultimately proved impossible to maintain this naval supremacy, so that while the system of passes severely hampered native shipping it did not make it altogether impossible, the far better equipped

From M. A. P. Meilink-Roelofsz, *Asian Trade and European Influence in the Indonesian Archipelago between 1500 and about 1630* (The Hague: Martinus Nijoff, 1962), pp. 120-22. Reprinted by permission of the publisher. Footnotes omitted.

northern Europeans did not adopt any different tactics. They too confined themselves mainly to the establishment of naval and military *points d'appui* from which they could keep a check on native trade and shipping and obstruct these as much as possible.

At the beginning of the sixteenth century the Portuguese concentration of power was not opposed by a united Asia, one of the very important reasons for the rapid success of the Portuguese. For that matter, the political and economic interests of the various countries did not run parallel in Europe either, but when the Portuguese introduced their policy of expansion European Christianity, in theory at least, was still intact. This fact restrained Venice, for example, from proceeding openly against Portugal in Asia and it also had an effect upon the conclusion of the pact between Spain and Portugal about the division of spheres of influence. The Reformation brought the schism here, too, and led to the activities of unscrupulous, northern European protestant competitors in Asia.

In Asia, apart from the division between the Moslem and the Hindu world, there were the divisions between the various trends and sects, of which those between the Sunnites and the Shi-ites were the most important. In her struggle against Sunnite Turkey, Portugal found an ally in Shi-ite Persia, and her attempts to destroy the trade monopoly of the Moslem merchants on the coast of India were supported by a large proportion of the Hindu population. The Portuguese supplied the Hindu rulers with firearms, and they imported horses from Arabia and Persia to the countries in southern India where these animals were not bred but where they were nevertheless indispensible to the Hindu rulers for resisting Moslem expansion on the Indian mainland. Because of this, the Maharajas became dependent upon the foreigners.

In the Malay-Indonesian area, too, closer relations were sought with the Hindu countries of Java. The Portuguese tried to get on a good footing with the Hindu merchants in this region, with the result that in the seaport of Malacca it was the Hindu element which promoted Portuguese settlement and which, after the conquest, occupied the foremost position in the commercial life of the port.

While Asia was so divided, there was great solidarity among the Portuguese and half-blood Portuguese, so that in spite of the vast distances and the loose structure of the empire, in times of danger the various Portuguese settlements came to one another's assistance. This solidarity was shared by the native converts to Christianity.

Even more serious for the Asians than their lack of unity was the fact that they had no naval power like that of the Portuguese. The war fleets of the Portuguese were something quite new in the Indian Ocean. The Asians were no strangers to marine warfare but most of their battles must have been fought quite near the coast, since they were occasioned by the necessity of warding off onslaughts from pirates or attacks from the sea. But the Asia of those days was unacquainted with trade carried on by armed merchantmen with the object of obtaining and maintaining a monopoly. Most of the transport and most of the trade in the valuable products destined for the West was in the hands of Moslems who, it is true, occupied a powerful position. But they owed this position entirely to their commercial relations and they too were divided by conflicting interests. They carried on their commercial traffic in unarmed, lightly-built craft, the planks of which were generally lashed together. These ships could not carry heavy armament. These were swift-sailing vessels designed to complete their voyages with the help of the periodically blowing monsoon winds. There was no powerfully centralized state authority behind this trade, nor did it have one clearly-defined aim. But the spiritual power of Islam endowed the Moslem world with great unity and strength. It made every Moslem merchant not only a follower of Islam but also a propagator of the doctrine and a defender of the faith. In the Indian Ocean and the Malay-Indonesian Archipelago, therefore, it was Islam which offered united opposition to the Portuguese. But of all the Moslem countries, Turkey as the only western Asian state was also the only one which possessed a war fleet anything like the technical equal of the European navies and artillery which was not inferior to that of the West. As for the other countries of Asia, even such a powerful kingdom as that reigned over by the Great Mogul did not possess a war fleet; in later days this ruler was partly dependent upon the Europeans for sea transport.

Religion and Commerce: Pretext and Motive?

Islam, then, had made good its influence in religious terms, had conquered lands and developed a staying power, to the discomfiture of politically effective Christians. May this suggest a possible disjunction between the religious and the political and economic

From Carlo M. Cipolla, *Guns and Sails in the Early Phase of European Expansion, 1400-1700* (London: Collins Publishers, 1965; New York: Random House, Inc. [Pantheon Books], 1965), pp. 132-38. © 1965 by Carlo M. Cipolla. Reprinted by permission of the publishers. Footnotes omitted.

drives? If, on the Islamic showing, a proselytizing spirit (and a resistance to proselytizing) may be effective without any corresponding political effectiveness (or if it may still be effective long after its association with political power), then the political effectiveness of Europe in the East need have no definitive connection with an aggressive religious impulse. Something else had to be there, for the Muslims had as much; they were often defeating Christians while Europeans were defeating "Moors."

Some of the things that were there—and that have already been mentioned, in earlier selections—were of course the economic motive and the fruits of economic advance. The Ottoman Turks, by their capture of Constantinople in 1453, had closed one of the old routes to China. Venice and Genoa, by these routes, had once enjoyed a monopoly of the eastern trade. Now Portugal, with its feats of navigation, might hope to supersede them.

When Vasco da Gama dropped anchor in the harbor of Calicut, a native asked what the Portuguese were looking for in Asia. The answer of da Gama allegedly was "Christians and spices." When Albuquerque attacked Malacca in 1511 he told his officers that they had to exert themselves to the utmost in the coming battle because of two reasons: "the great service we shall perform to our Lord in casting the Moors out of the country and quenching the fire of the sect of Mahomet . . . and the service we shall render to the King Dom Manoel in taking this city because it is the source of all the spiceries and drugs." Bernal Diaz, speculating about the motives that had driven him and his like to the Indies, wrote that they had left Europe "to serve God and his Majesty, to give light to those who were in the darkness and to grow rich as all men desire to do."

Through the idea of mission and crusade the conquistadores succeeded where the medieval merchants failed and were able to reconcile the antithesis between business and religion that had plagued the conscience of medieval Europe. One has no reason to doubt the sincerity of their statements, but one may wonder about their realism and the validity of their rationalizations. That the Europeans were more often than not imbued with religious zeal and intolerance is a fact that does not need to be proven. But it is doubtful whether the religious element was as relevant among the motives that drove people overseas as it was among the forces that helped them once they were there. Religious convictions nourished boldness in battle, endurance through ordeals, truculence after victory. But, missionaries apart, when the Europeans undertook the perilous journey, they were dreaming more about Mammon than about lost souls to enlighten. Ogier Ghiselin de Busbecq, the sixteenth-century diplomat, was an inveterate pessimist, but he cannot have been far from the truth when he wrote that for the "expeditions [to the Indies and the Antipodes] religion supplies the pretext and gold the motive."

European expansion after 1400 can hardly be depicted as an extension of the Crusades. It cannot be described as the result of Malthusian pressures either. Recurrent epidemics were constantly checking population growth and no population pressure of any relevance was felt in Europe till the second half of the eighteenth century. On the other hand the number of Europeans overseas remained very exiguous until the nineteenth century. Those who left Europe were few. Those who arrived at their destination were half as many. And a large proportion of those who survived the ordeals of the journey and the dangers of life overseas returned to Europe as soon as they could.

European expansion was essentially a commercial venture, and the fact that the colonial policies of the European powers had a very pronounced mercantile tone was the natural consequence of the basic motives behind that expansion. King François I of France was flippantly rude when he styled King Manoel of Portugal *"le roi épicier"* but he was historically correct. One may only add that the States General of Holland and the rulers of England and Spain were no less favorably inclined to "grocery" than Dom Manoel.

A wide range of economic opportunities magnetized the Europeans overseas. The spice trade, of course, always gave promise of lucrative results. But there was more than that. The Portuguese became increasingly interested in the spice trade toward the end of the fifteenth century. Earlier in the century they crept along the African coast looking for ivory, ebony, slaves, gold, grain, and fish. In the sixteenth and seventeenth centuries, when the Europeans had established themselves in the Indian Ocean and the China seas, they did not limit themselves to the spice trade. They were at that time interested in a wide range of commodities from saltpeter to copper, silk, and porcelain. The current textbooks of economic history are wrong when they give the impression that the only activity of the European adventurers in Asia was that of supplying the West with Eastern products. The Portuguese, the Dutch, and the English were the middlemen in a vast network of commercial activity among Asian nations and a good deal of European imports were actually paid for with the income derived from invisible exports of shipping and commercial services. Opportunities were many, risks high but profits higher.

Religion supplied the pretext and gold the motive. The technological progress accomplished by Atlantic Europe during the fourteenth and fifteenth centuries provided the means. . . . The "motives" were already active in the Mediterranean Europe as early as the thirteenth century. The Italians and the Catalans were economically very advanced but they did not succeed in outflanking the Moslem blockade because they were not supported by adequate technology. They made some use of the energy of the wind and later that of gunpowder, but only in a subsidiary way. Essentially they relied on human muscular energy for movement and fighting. But a crew could hardly master the ocean by the use of muscular energy, and when confronted with an enemy it had to yield to superior numbers if the fight were decided by a final melee. The link between the Mediterranean and Atlantic developments was Columbus. He had to borrow "Atlantic vessels, Biscayan sailors, and Portuguese nautical techniques." His role and relevance through the genesis of the project was that of agent of Genoese capital. The contribution of the Mediterranean world to European expansion at the end of the fifteenth century was financial and commercial rather than technological.

The gunned ship developed by Atlantic Europe in the course of the fourteenth and fifteenth centuries was the contrivance that made possible the European saga. It was essentially a compact device that allowed a relatively small crew to master unparalleled masses of inanimate energy for movement and destruction. The secret of the sudden and rapid European ascendancy was all there: in the skill acquired by Atlantic nations in the use of the sailing ships and in their having understood that "sea fight in these days come seldome to boarding or to great execution of bows, arrows, small shot, and the sword but are chiefly performed by the great artillery."

When the sailing vessels of Atlantic Europe arrived, hardly anything could resist them. As Albuquerque proudly wrote to his King in 1513, "at the rumor of our coming the [native] ships all vanished and even the birds ceased to skim over the water." This was not rhetorical prose. Within fifteen years after their first arrival in Indian waters the Portuguese had completely destroyed the naval power of the Arabs and their King could justifiably style himself "Lord of the Conquest, Navigation, and Commerce of Ethiopia, Arabia, Persia, and India." Meanwhile business and technology were rapidly advancing in Europe and before the non-Europeans had absorbed the shock of the first contact with the Atlantic vessels, more efficient and more numerous vessels arrived. The caravels and the carracks were followed by the galleons. The Portuguese fleets were followed by the vastly more formidable fleets of the Dutch and the English. The arrival of the new invaders coincided with the outbreak of bloody struggles among the whites. But if the Europeans were tragically divided, their opponents were often no more united and they proved unable to take full advantage of the fratricidal quarrels of the Europeans.

In the last analysis, it is not the sincerity of the proselytizing spirit that remains in question—it is the sufficiency. The economic motif, usually intertwined with even the most edifying accounts, suggests an ultimately secular complex of reasons for expansion or non-expansion. And proximately, in the next section, we have other shades of "spirit" to examine.

III / "SPIRIT"

In *The Decline of the West* Oswald Spengler located his "Faustian man" in Europe. No part of Asian history spoke to him of the stormer of heavens or the world-seeker, the chooser of a quest: Schopenhauer had diffused too well the theme of Asian world-denial. Tennyson (perhaps reflecting, not Schopenhauer, but Hume on the virtues of conflict and motion in divided Europe) chose his "twenty years of Europe" over "a cycle of Cathay." (By this reckoning, the fall and non-revival of Rome would be a stimulating blessing, while in China, after the fall of Han in the third century A.D., the recurrent revival of empire would be a monolithic, stultifying curse). The noble fate of Tennyson's "Ulysses" was "to strive, to seek, to find, and not to yield." Others, too (as the next selection illustrates), have considered Europe unique, its history uniquely vital and expansive, because of its Faustian or Homeric spirit, which was ostensibly inherent.

10 / WESTERN VIEWS OF EUROPEAN SPIRIT VERSUS ASIAN SPIRIT

European Society

. . . Having made the world, she [i.e., Europe] has lost it. The world has rebelled against her in the name of those very values of liberty, justice, and equality for all nations, and of respect for the individual whosoever he be, which she herself formulated and propagated without thought of the consequences. So we see her

From Denis de Rougemont, *The Meaning of Europe* (London: Sidgwick & Jackson Ltd., 1963), pp. 24-5, 27. Reprinted by permission of Sidgwick & Jackson Ltd., Stein and Day, Inc., and Editions de la Baconniere.

again reduced to herself, confined within the boundaries of her Asian promontory and no larger, let us note carefully, than she was in the Middle Ages. She is still the heart of a West born of her deeds, but in which two great empires are challenging her supremacy, one hostilely, the other as an ally, whilst Africa, Asia, and the Arab world endeavor to deploy their renascent strength against the divided West.

Is this the end of the West's Adventure? If so, what it amounts to is that the West made the world, but made it hostile to its makers.

Before even attempting a reply to this question with all its burning topicality, we shall try to summarize the constant characteristics of the European phenomenon . . . and of the spirit which has sustained through the centuries the astonishing dynamism of the West.

To my mind, the passion inspiring this unprecedented adventure is best symbolized by one of the heroes of the oldest Greek poem; I refer to Homer's Ulysses, the central character in the *Odyssey*.

His departure on a species of crusade against Troy, a town in the Near East, in order to save the honor of the West and to recapture Helen, symbol of virtue and beauty, prefigures the missionary ideal which, between fifteen hundred and two thousand years later, was to move the early Church to send out evangelists as far as China to the East and to Iceland and the Atlantic coasts of America to the West. The military victory of the Greeks over the Trojans prefigures the military expeditions of Europeans to the four other continents. That is the *Iliad,* a "poem about power" as Simone Weil aptly called it. But the most typically Western thing about the Homeric poems is what followed: Ulysses' personal adventure described in the *Odyssey,* that interminable voyage toward original, eternal wisdom, toward his native country of Ithaca; this enthralling tale of a wanderer, these endless peregrinations which were also a prolonged "error" in the Latin and English meaning of the word. For everything that happens throughout this long epic suggests that Ulysses, a brave and resourceful man, secretly prefers the voyage to its destination, the trials of the journey to a blessed arrival, and the never-ending risks to happiness and peace with Penelope. To conquer the elements, to measure his strength against visible and invisible adversaries, to penetrate ever further into the unknown, skilfully guiding his ship between opposite excesses—the Scillas and Charibdis—this is Ulysses' master-passion, and this too was to be the guiding passion of the great creators of Western culture. Western man is the man who always goes farther, beyond the limits set by nature, beyond traditions fixed by his ancestors, even beyond himself—*on to adventure*! . . .

• • •

The essence of the genius of the West, which most clearly illustrates the contrast between the adventurous Western half of the world and the metaphysical genius of the East, is its preference for the ardent pursuit of partial truths, *come what may*—and for creative risk-taking over prudent meditation on immutable wisdom.

A Representative Asian Society

As a more sober assessment of "spirit," here is one for a specific area. Unlike the preceding selection, this statement about Asian "spirit" (or a branch of it), in implied comparison with the European, is not a manifesto.

. . . The general *Weltanschauung*, the world-view, of this Javanese court culture, . . . is difficult to put in a nutshell. Basically it was transcendental, what Max Weber has called other-worldly, directed towards the attainment of harmony—you will recognize the elements of Indian thought—of harmony between the external world, the cosmos, and the earth, between nature and the human being, between the universe of the gods and the universe of man, of balance among the various elements within the human soul. These determinants of Javanese thinking, feeling, and religious speculation have survived virtually intact to this very day. Alien to this kind of world view are sharp and rigid confrontations, as is also any concern with the world of harsh matter. That is not to say, of course, that the Javanese did not have to deal with confrontations or with the world of harsh matter; but as far as the prevailing ideology was concerned, these things were despised and shunned. This was why, e.g., trade and commerce, being of this world, were intrinsically thought and taught to be alien to the spirit I have described, why it was left to the foreigner to "dirty" his hands with them, while the Javanese, insofar as they were concerned with trade, merely regulated it to keep it in balance, so to speak.

From Harry J. Benda, "Continuity and Change in Indonesian Islam," *Asian and African Studies* (Annual of the Israel Oriental Society), I (1965), 127-8. Reprinted by permission of *Asian and African Studies*.

11 / TWO MODERN CHINESE VIEWS

*De Rougemont and Benda are writing in different veins, the differ-
ence between an emotional tract and a scholarly perception. The
former is a tract for the times, and de Rougemont sees the times
as a period of eclipse of European power—or he sees others assuming this, and he reacts with a spirited (and "spirit") defense.
Interestingly enough, there have been Asian voices raised, too, in
similar vein, emotional reactions to allegations of weakness; but
the allegations were made by the speakers themselves.*

A Prescription

*Here is the famous Chinese writer, Lu Hsün (1881-1936), reacting
to a request that he recommend a reading list for Chinese youth
(1925):*

I have never studied this problem; so I cannot answer.

But I want to take this opportunity to say something of my own
experience for the benefit of the readers.

Whenever I read Chinese books, I feel that I quiet down, that I
am being separated from life. When I read foreign books—Indian
books excepted—I feel often a closer contact with life. I feel an
urge to do something.

There are indeed Chinese books which speak for taking an active
part in life, but that is only the optimism of a vampire. Foreign
books may also inspire dejection and pessimism, but that is the
dejection and pessimism of living human beings.

My advice is therefore not to read any Chinese books, or to read
as few as you can. But read more foreign books.

If you do not read Chinese books, you will end up in being unable to write. But what modern youth needs is not to write, but to
act. If you remain a living human being, it does not really matter
if you cannot write.

A Description

At about the same time another Chinese writer, though much more

Quoted in T. A. Hsia, "Aspects of the Power of Darkness in Lu Hsün," *The
Journal of Asian Studies*, XXIII, No. 2 (February 1964), 196-97. Reprinted by
permission of *The Journal of Asian Studies*. Footnote omitted.

From Wen-Han Kiang, *The Chinese Student Movement* (New York: King's
Crown Press, 1948), pp. 42-3. Reprinted by permission of the publisher. Footnotes omitted.

sympathetic than Lu Hsün to what they both saw as the Chinese spirit, made some similar generalizations.

Liang Sou-ming defined civilization as a way of life, and life as the unfolding of an unlimited will. In accordance with this definition, he outlined three types of civilizations in the world. First, there is the Western civilization, the basic spirit of which is a "forward-moving will." Science, democracy, and the desire to conquer nature, all are derived from this will. Secondly, there is the Chinese civilization, the basic spirit of which is characterized by the will to contentment, harmony, and the golden mean. Thirdly, there is the Indian civilization, the basic spirit of which is the will to withdrawal and retreat. By Indian civilization, Liang Sou-ming referred primarily to Buddhism.

According to Liang Sou-ming, the thing that differentiates the three civilizations is the way in which they solve the problems of living. The Western civilization represents the original or native tendency of man. It always pushes forward to get what it desires and to reconstruct the situation in order to satisfy its desires. In other words, it is the attitude of struggle. The genius of Chinese civilization is not to look forward but sidewise. When confronted with a problem, it does not aim at changing the situation but attempts to readjust its own desires to gain harmony. The Indian civilization tends to cancel both the problem and the desires. It turns backward because there is no wish either to change the situation or to readjust its own desires. This is the road to asceticism.

12 / A CHINESE COMMUNIST VIEW

Chinese Communists, too, in some of their references to early Chinese culture, dwell on the theme of passive spirit. "Struggle" and "contradiction" are the watchwords of the Chinese Communist revolution. In its intellectual aspects the revolution, domestically, was directed in part against the old ideal of harmony.

The Communists would never call themselves "Faustian" (though Kuo Mo-jo, a well-known Communist scholar and writer, translated Goethe's Faust, *Part One, in his younger, pre-Communist days).*

From Donald J. Munro, "Chinese Communist Treatment of the Thinkers of the Hundred Schools Period," *The China Quarterly,* No. 24 (October-December 1965), 134-36. Reprinted by permission of *The China Quarterly.* Footnotes omitted.

Not Goethe but Marx, with his adaptation of Hegelian dialectic, is the Chinese Communists' first Western source of inspiration. But the dialectic, with its image of struggle between thesis and antithesis to the resolution of synthesis—and then its setting up of the synthesis as a new thesis in a new or continuing struggle—is an abstract version, for the goddess History, of the Faustian personal demon. Striving, driving, is indispensable. Occasionally Chinese Communist scholars, in a vein of cultural nationalism, have claimed to discern the spirit of dialectical struggle in one or another of the old schools of Chinese philosophy. But more characteristically, as the next selection reports, the Communists have disparaged these schools as soporific.

Of the Chinese philosophers mentioned in this selection, Lao-tzu (traditional birthdate, 604 B.C.) and Chuang-tzu (fourth century B.C.) were, respectively, the putative founder and the most famous follower of the doctrines of Taoism. Though Taoism, a protean body of thought and intuition, took on associations with proto-science and popular rebellions, and therefore has its share of honor in the Chinese heritage (as the Communists selectively construct it), its quietistic philosophical side fails to meet the test of struggle.

The Mohist school referred to here is the school of Mo Ti or Mo-tzu (fl. between 479 and 381 B.C.), who adumbrated a system of logic (deficient, according to the Communists), and who advocated "universal love" (obviously uncongenial, as sentimental idealism, to dialectical materialists).

Mencius 372-289 B.C.), after Confucius, was the most famous classical exponent of Confucianism.

The Ch'eng-Chu school was the so-called Neo-Confucian li-hsüeh school that came into prominence in the Sung period and remained the orthodox version of Confucianism until the twentieth century. The brothers Ch'eng Hao (1032-1085) and Ch'eng I (1033-1107) were leading developers of Neo-Confucian doctrine, and Chu Hsi (1130-1200) was the supreme synthesizer and systematizer of the school.

The failure to understand the nature of struggle between opposites is most clearly manifest in the rudimentary dialectical views of the early thinkers. This points to a unique deficiency in the Chinese legacy. In Western thought from the earliest times there was such an understanding. Heraclitus spoke of *strife* between opposites as essential to the coming into being of things and to ordered change. Such an idea found its way into the idealism of Hegel and thence to Marx.

Kuan Feng and Lin Yu-shih hold that dialectics and idealistic philosophies are basically contradictory, for dialectics means constant development through the clash of opposites, while in an idealism such as that of Lao Tzu all opposition disappears in the Absolute. There is no development and change in Tao through the clash of opposites. A host of modern commentators offer variations on the interpretation that Lao Tzu's dialectic seeks to eliminate all struggle between opposites. Chuang Tzu is said to carry the denial of struggle even farther to the point of seeming to deny the existence of opposites. His dialectics become an attempt to avoid contradictions. He preferred to take a middle position between opposites (e.g., between good and bad, strength and weakness) as an expedient means for preserving life. Or he would make a "head in the sand" escape from conflict by "transcending" it with a flight into "absolute freedom" or "pure experience."

Not only Taoistic dialectical theories lack an understanding of struggle. The dialectics of the Mohist school are restricted to explaining the contradictions between phenomena and to elaborating on a logical rule for analyzing them. There is no conception of struggle between opposites resulting in development.

The Chinese tendency to avoid struggle or to seek some compromise is not a new discovery of the Chinese Communists. It was recognized by certain figures connected with the cultural readjustment associated with the May 4th Movement of 1917-21. For example, in a joint statement, Hu Shih, pupil of John Dewey and proselytiser of pragmatism in China, and Ch'en Tu-hsiu, one of the founders of the Chinese Communist Party, said:

> The old literature, old politics, and old ethics have always belonged to one family; we cannot abandon one and preserve the others. It is Oriental to compromise and only go halfway when reforming, for fear of opposition. This was the most important factor behind the failures of reform movements during the last several decades.

But the negative aspects of China's philosophical legacy have left special problems for the Chinese leadership, which is eager both to promote a politically conscious populace and to rid the country of the ideological dross of the past. These special problems are recognized by philosophers observing their own countrymen. In their eyes, early attempts to transcend conflict by entering the realm of "absolute freedom" where all problems disappear have their counterpart today in the "Ah Q" * spirit of so many Chinese who try to rationalize problems away. The Taoist preference for taking a mean position between opposites is seen today in "middle-of-the-roadism," by which people hope to avoid the possibility of making a mistake. The attempt to deny opposites was handed down from the early period to the present by feudal rulers who found it a useful tool for drugging the people; those who believe there is no difference between life and death, between getting and losing, will not struggle to achieve the former. Liu Chieh, whose ideas are derived from Mencius and the Ch'eng-Chu school, states that man must not take part in "wild and wrong acts" which may injure Heaven and damage reason, but must strive to recover his heavenly nature. In other words, man's task is to devote himself to internal examination and avoid struggle.

13 / THE CHINESE IN SOUTHEAST ASIA: EXPANSIONIST DEEDS WITHOUT THE WILL

How do such specimens of Chinese thinking, running across almost the whole spectrum from devotees of "Chinese spirit" to materialist revolutionaries, relate to the problem of expansion, the European example and the Asian counter-example? It is noteworthy that Chinese settled in Southeast Asia before the Europeans came, but the Chinese made no political impact. The following group of extracts refers to this.

A Nationalist's Lament

In the first decade of the twentieth century the reformer, Liang Ch'i-ch'ao (1873-1929), tried to inculcate an ebullient nationalism in the Chinese people. He wrote about earlier vital Chinese spirits (alas, he felt, untypical); and he pointed to the paradox of a Chinese colonization of lands that Western powers, not China at all, then forcibly made into colonies.

. . . [Liang Ch'i-ch'ao] told the stories of the Han Dynasty's wide-roaming Chang Ch'ien and Pan Ch'ao and asked for the revivification of their spirit; for, said Liang, if China stays torpid, she will

---

* The antihero of Lu Hsün's famous "Our Story of Ah Q," which inveighed against what the author saw as typical Chinese hypocritical passivity—ED.

From Joseph R. Levenson, *Liang Ch'i-ch'ao and the Mind of Modern China* (London: Thames and Hudson, 1959), pp. 123-24. Reprinted by permission of the author and publisher. Footnotes omitted.

simply be bait for Teutonic imperialists. Likewise, he devoted other articles, half tribute and half warning, to praise of Yuan Ch'ung-huan (1584-1630), a Ming general in the wars against the Manchus —Liang calls him China's greatest soldier—Cheng Ho, the famous fifteenth-century navigator, and Chinese emigrant-colonizers who had crossed the Pacific to settle new lands. Liang lamented the fact that after Columbus and Vasco da Gama came many other great Western sailors, but there had never been a second Cheng Ho, and he pointed up the disgrace of Western domination over countries largely settled by yellow races. Chinese had broken the ground for colonization, and now they were only as "oxen and horses." The English and the Dutch rule now where Chinese had led the way.

Chinese, Portuguese, and Dutch in the Moluccas: The Chinese Declare "No Contest"

"Oxen and horses" . . . *dumb, patient submitters to the yoke. It was certainly true that China as an organized society had shown no interest in its expansion overseas, no sense of "national purpose" to expand. But elements of the Chinese population had emigrated overseas from China. Here is a pertinent excerpt from the dynastic history of the Ming (1368-1644).*

The Moluccas are situated in the southeastern ocean and have a reputation of being wealthy. When their chief goes out he has a great state, and his subjects, who meet him, lay down at the side of the road with folded hands.

There is an incense-mountain, and when it has rained the incense falls down and covers the ground in such quantities that the people cannot collect it all. Their chief stores up large quantities, in order to sell it to the merchant-vessels that visit this place. It is the only country in the eastern sea which produces cloves, which are useful for dispelling bad humors, and therefore Chinese merchants go in large numbers to trade there.

During the period Wan-li (1573-1619) the Franks [Portuguese] came to attack this country; the chief was overcome in battle and offered his submission, on which they pardoned him and put him again on the throne; they imposed an annual tribute of cloves

From W. P. Groeneveldt, *Historical Notes on Indonesia and Malaya, Compiled from Chinese Sources* (Djakarta: C. V. Bhratara, 1960), pp. 117-18. Originally published in the *Venhaudelingen van het Bataviaasch Genootschap van Kunsten en Wetenscheffen*, Vol. XXXIX, 1880. Reprinted by permission of the publisher. Footnotes omitted.

and then went away, without leaving soldiers in charge of the place.

Afterwards the [Dutch] red-haired barbarians came across the sea and knowing that the Portuguese had gone away, they availed themselves of the occasion and went to the town, where they took the chief and said to him: if you serve us well, we will be your masters, and we can beat the Portuguese. The chief had no choice, he obeyed and continued to govern his country.

When the Portuguese heard this, they became very angry and collected soldiers to attack them, but these were killed on their way by the Chinese, as is told in the history of Manila. The Dutch now, though they kept the Moluccas, went away every year or every two years and then came back again. In the meantime the son of the Portuguese chief had succeeded his father; he wanted to carry out his plans and came with a large force for this purpose. Now it happened that the Dutch were absent at that time, so he conquered the Moluccas, killed the chief, and put a man on the throne whom he trusted. Not long afterwards the Dutch came again, they also took the town, drove away the chief who had been put up by the Portuguese and raised to the throne the son of the former chief. After this time they fought every year and many people were killed, till the Chinese who lived there talked to both sides, advising them to stop fighting and rather to divide the country; on this the high mountain of Banda was taken as boundary, the north of this mountain going to the Dutch and the south to the Portuguese; it became a little more quiet now and the Moluccas remained divided between the two countries.

Chinese and Spaniards in the Philippines

"The Chinese who lived there talked to both sides. . . ." The Chinese who lived at home, directing the Chinese Empire, showed no interest in extending the empire to places of Chinese settlement overseas. And the Chinese overseas would advise "the Portuguese and the Dutch"—or anyone else but the Chinese—"to divide the country" and rule. Was this the counter-Ulysses spirit at work: always ready not to take the oars, not to strive, not to seek, not to find, just to yield?

As the next excerpt indicates, the Chinese abroad did not always yield lightly, for there might be local revolts against the oc-

From Edgar Wickberg, *The Chinese in Philippine Life, 1850-1898* (New Haven and London: Yale University Press, 1965), pp. 3-6, 209-212, 234, 243. Reprinted by permission of the publisher. Footnotes omitted.

cupying power. But the revolts came because the Chinese state, until modern times, was somnolent where the overseas Chinese were concerned. Probably at no time were there as many Spaniards as Chinese in the Philippines; and the mandarin was at least as proud as the hidalgo. But the mandarin stayed at home, dismissing his compatriots overseas as poor in spirit, and seeming to be poor in spirit himself (from an expansionist's point of view) as he dismissed the idea of a Chinese flag following Chinese trade.

Long before 1850 the Chinese had been significantly involved in the economic and social affairs of the Philippines. Direct contact between China and the Philippines existed from at least the Sung period (960-1279). By Ming times (1368-1644) the *tung-yang chen-lu,* or eastern route of the Chinese junk trading system, had been established, passing through the western side of the Philippine archipelago enroute from South China to Sulu, Borneo, and the Moluccas. Through the junk trade several points in the Philippines enjoyed regular commercial and cultural contacts with the Chinese. Passengers on the junks, whether merchants or otherwise, occasionally settled in various parts of the Philippines, at least on a temporary basis. But nothing is known about how such settlers may have fitted into the economic and social life of their host societies. At Jolo, in the archipelago of Sulu, an important trading center for the raw products of neighboring regions, there were a Chinese wharf and lodging quarter. In the Manila area, the Spanish conquerors of 1570 found a small settlement of about 150 Chinese. But no other information is available about these settlements or the existence of other Chinese colonies.

The arrival of the Spanish conquerors in the Philippines in the 1560s meant new opportunities for the Chinese. In Fukien province, on China's southeastern coast, shipowning merchants immediately realized the potential economic significance of the newly-developing Manila galleon trade between the Philippines and Mexico. The way was open for Chinese vessels to carry goods from China to Manila, there to be loaded for markets in Mexico. The Spaniards, unlike the Portuguese, possessed no trading station on the China coast. Nor did they handle the China-Manila carrying trade in their own vessels. Instead, they developed a pattern of waiting for the yearly monsoon winds to bring the Chinese junks to Manila, bearing silks and other luxury goods from China to be transshipped to Mexico on the Manila galleon. On the galleon's return voyage Mexican silver was brought to Manila, from whence it was taken to China by the Chinese junk traders in repayment for the luxury goods they had brought. Both the Chinese and the Manila Spaniards, who acted as middlemen, profited enormously from this arrangement.

Shipowning merchants were not the only Chinese who came to the Philippines. Soon other Chinese—merchants and artisans— were migrating to the archipelago, attracted by the sophisticated economy newly established at Manila and other centers of Spanish residence. The provisioning of the Spanish settlements with needed goods and services was an open field for Chinese enterprise. Not only merchants and artisans but fishermen and market gardeners settled in the Manila area and supplied the needs of the Spaniards. By 1603, barely thirty-two years after the founding of Manila as a Spanish settlement, the Chinese population there was estimated at 20,000—in contrast to perhaps 1,000 Spaniards. Even before that, the Chinese had achieved a virtual monopoly in the retail commercial and industrial life of this settlement and were moving in the same direction in the other parts of the archipelago where Spaniards had established themselves.

.   .   .

The Philippine Chinese appeal to China for consular protection in 1880 was the first known attempt by their community to es- tablish a political relationship with China. Their action may be attributed both to their insecurity, in light of events in the Philip- pines, and to their awareness of the response that could be ex- pected from China. The fact that such a request was made reflected changes in the Philippines, both inside and outside the Chinese community. That it was made with any hope of a favorable re- sponse from China was due to consciousness of China's changing attitude toward the overseas Chinese.

.   .   .

But the decisive reason for the petition was simply an awareness that intervention by China was possible and that it produced good results. In 1880 the efficacy of China's intervention in over- seas Chinese matters had but recently been demonstrated in an amelioration of coolie labor recruiting practices and an improve- ment in the condition of Chinese coolies in Cuba. The fact that the latter case involved Spain was a pointed lesson to the Philip- pine Chinese that Spain could be made to yield if China inter- vened. Therefore, the timing of the Philippine Chinese consulate request was dictated not merely by the promulgation of a new Spanish tax law (contribución industrial, 1878), and the development of an anti-Chinese campaign in the Philippines, but also the recent evidence that China could successfully negotiate with Spain.

China's aroused interest in the overseas Chinese dated only from the 1860s. The traditional Chinese view that overseas emigration was, at best, of no concern to Chinese officialdom had been evident in China's unwillingness to act in response to the loss of "unfilial" Chinese lives abroad. . . . [In] the letter of a Fukien official in 1605, answering a Spanish letter which justified the 1603 massacre of Chinese in Manila, the Chinese official said that overseas Chinese, as deserters of the tombs of their ancestors, were unworthy of China's protection. A similar answer is attributed to a Chinese official in 1740, when the Dutch wrote from the Netherlands Indies to explain their massacre of Chinese during that year. This official is supposed to have expressed a lack of sympathy for those who would abandon their ancestors in quest of money.

Other traditional attitudes—that overseas migrants were likely to include political dissidents who were to be feared, and that it was better to attract foreign traders to China under the aegis of the Chinese tributary system than to let Chinese carry the trade abroad—found expression in an imperial edict of 1712, forbidding Chinese to trade and reside in Southeast Asia. Five years later another edict allowed those already abroad to come home without fear of punishment. But in 1729 still another edict announced that a date must be set after which those overseas would not be allowed to return. Despite these edicts, and the harsh penalties registered in the Ch'ing dynasty law code, the *Ta-Ch'ing lü-li*, little was done to prevent Chinese from going abroad. Since the laws were neither rescinded nor enforced they provided a fruitful source of extorted funds for local officials whenever a wealthy Chinese returned from abroad.

This condition began to change in the 1860s. The first indication was a clause in the Chinese peace treaty with Britain in 1860, which acknowledged the right of Chinese to go to British colonies, sail on British ships for that purpose, and make contracts with British subjects to that end. Eight years later, in the Burlingame Treaty with the United States, China acknowledged the general right of its citizens to leave the country. Within ten years after that time the Chinese had begun to establish consulates abroad, one purpose of which was to protect the lives and property of overseas Chinese.

• • •

One looks in vain for any evidences of a philosophical Pan-Sinism in the writings of Chinese officials of this period. The overseas Chinese communities were considered worthy of protection not because they were little bits of China scattered about the globe, but because they were merchant communities whose earnings— and perhaps "knowhow"—were suddenly of value to China's "self-strengthening" effort. There was, of course, very little about these communities that was culturally attractive to a Chinese official. They were colonial communities whose leading elements were merchants, not scholar-officials. Given the absence of nationalism and the presence of traditional Chinese social values, and granting the mercantile nature of overseas Chinese society at that time, it is not surprising that China's official interest took this form.

• • •

In the seventeenth and eighteenth centuries the Spanish could massacre Chinese in the Philippines with the knowledge that even though Fukien and Kwangtung officials might be concerned, there would be no large-scale retaliation from the Chinese government. But in the late nineteenth century the Spaniards were aware of China's new interest in the overseas Chinese, and Spanish consciousness of China's developing naval strength acted as a deterrent to reckless action.

From the Chinese side, the revolts of the seventeenth century were made in the knowledge that the only help the Philippine Chinese might get would come from Chinese adventurers. No aid was to be expected from China. One of the reasons for such revolts was precisely the impossibility of aid from China, which made drastic methods the only course of action. In the nineteenth-century context, revolts were unnecessary because China's aid was available.

14 / THE SOCIAL CONTEXT OF THE IMPULSE TO EXPAND

"Poor in spirit (from an expansionist's point of view). . . ." But why should spirit be assessed conclusively from any particular

*point of view? And why should such an assessment be taken as an
ultimate explanation of a particular course of non-activity—in
this case, non-expansion? From the Confucian mandarin point of
view the concepts of flag and fellow-nationals were for a very long
time nonexistent. It is an anachronism to speak of a Chinese national
purpose, or of a concept of national solidarity during the age of
European expansion. It was not a case of a weak purpose being
overborne by strong ones. It was a case, rather, of very different
purposes, from different structures of societies. If China's relation
to the Philippines' Chinese was changing in the nineteenth century, this was because far-reaching changes were taking place in
China. They reached farther than relations with the Philippines—
and they affected much more than temper or spirit.*

*Sir George Sansom suggests this in the next pair of extracts when
he begins by comparing Europe to China and India for their respective "expansive impulses"—begins, indeed, with that familiar
reference to the energetic legacy of Greece—but touches on the
social context of "impulse." And when he treats sixteenth-century
Japan, he finds it quite as exuberant as Elizabethan England with
its great captains. Yet Japan withdrew in the seventeenth century
to isolation, while England went on around the world to colonize
and to make other countries colonies of England. The Japanese
spirit, it seems, had been willing too, so we have to look for something else to find what diverted it. Indeed, all the "spirits"—and
all the religions and the states of technology—exist in their own*
gestalts, *in their various complexes and contexts, social, economic,
and political.*

Greece, China, and India

European historians detect the first sign of [the divergence between Asian agrarian, relatively static societies and European mercantile, dynamic societies] from the ancient pattern in the city-
states of the Aegean Sea. For a number of reasons, all of which
are not clear but which mostly have to do with geography and
climate, this region developed new cultures differing somewhat
among themselves but all in striking contrast to the old. While,
for instance, in China and India of the first millennium B.C. there
were great stationary populations tilling vast areas of land, on
those small islands and promontories washed by Mediterranean

Sir George B. Sansom, *The Western World and Japan* (London, The Cresset
Press, Ltd., 1950). pp. 6-9, 15-17. Reprinted by permission of the publisher.
Footnote ommitted.

waters there lived peoples who could scarcely subsist upon the produce of their own soil but were obliged, by circumstance and temperament, to traffic freely overseas. This maritime trade, as it grew, brought into being a new social class of merchants, ship-builders, navigators, and other specialists upon whom the prosperity of their community largely depended. They were not numerous, but they were important. Maritime trade brought as much benefit as agriculture, so that the merchant rivaled the landlord in wealth and influence. There was now interposed between the traditional landlord-ruler and the passive peasant-serf an active middle class, with special interests of its own which inevitably gave it special political power. From such origins there developed in the great age of Greece—during the fifth and the fourth centuries B.C.—a new type of society dominated by concepts of political and economic freedom, devoted to navigation, colonization, and trade and active in the study of mathematics, astronomy, geography, and kindred sciences. This, despite its fluctuating fortunes in subsequent history, is the forerunner of that element in European life which has produced its characteristic political and social features—democratic principles of government, individualist doctrines, and the spirit of scientific enquiry.

It may be argued that the great Asiatic communities also had considerable commerce within themselves and with one another; that their merchants also undertook extensive journeys by land and by sea; and therefore that the political importance of trade in the Hellenic world is not exceptional. But the significance of the merchant in the Aegean city-states lay not so much in the length of his journeys or the volume of his trade as in his relative importance to a small community, in his status as a citizen. The great Asiatic communities were in general self-supporting and self-contained. Trade within their own frontiers was of importance because of their size, and there was often an extensive traffic between the various parts of great countries like China, where for example the products of widely-separated provinces would be exchanged by long overland or coastal journeys. But flourishing as this internal trade may have been, it was ancillary to the agriculture which provided the life-blood of the state. It was an extension of the agrarian economy, not a rival to it. The trader, therefore, did not as a rule achieve in these communities any outstanding social or political importance. In most of them indeed he was despised and oppressed by the ruling class. The merchant and the artisan usually ranked below the farmer in the social scale. The town was more important than the country only insofar as it was the seat of government and the center to which revenue flowed. Even in those countries or regions which, being favorably placed for overseas traffic, developed a considerable seaborne foreign trade, the shipowner, the shipbuilder, and the specialists upon whom they depended attained only a local or subsidiary importance. Here a useful illustration is provided by Chinese history. It shows a long and distinguished record of maritime commerce, particularly between ports in southern China and the Indian Ocean, going back possibly as far as the later Han and reaching its zenith under the early Ming emperors, who seem to have had some inkling of the importance of seapower. But in general it is true to say that Chinese maritime enterprise stemmed from no national impulse and received no consistent benefit of national policy. Until the nineteenth century the diplomatic and military effort of China was directed almost entirely across her land frontiers. The great movements of Chinese expansion progressed mainly overland to the west, while her defensive movements were pointed to her northern borders. She rarely faced seaward, because there was no circumstance obliging her to increase her naval strength or her seaborne trade for truly national purposes. No serious or continuing danger threatened her from the sea, and her own domestic economy was so massive and self-sufficient that foreign commerce was little more than a means of obtaining luxuries or curiosities to satisfy the whims of courtiers and high officials.

What has been said of China in these respects is true also of India. Indian ships made long voyages in classical times, for from the earliest recorded history we know of traders sending freight westward across the Indian Ocean to Africa and eastward to China. Indeed by the beginning of the Christian era Indian peoples had already begun a considerable enterprise of colonization which later extended as far as Malaya and Cambodia. Nevertheless, "in all the earlier ages India looked inward, not outward." In subsequent history also, time after time the expansive impulse fails, and Indian life turns in upon itself. It is not sensibly affected by influences from across the sea, and even alien conquerors pouring in across the land frontiers cannot change its essential nature though they may modify its outward forms.

This relative unimportance of foreign relations in the life of the great settled communities of Asia is but one expression of their self-sufficiency, for in general their history shows that, just as they have felt no great need of foreign merchandise, so they have been under no inner compulsion to seek wisdom or knowledge outside their own borders. Seen in this aspect China and India appear as prime examples of the characteristic Asiatic culture upon which a great uniform peasant population confers an independence and stability in strong contrast to the active, experimental temper of the cultures of the West. It is doubtless this contrast which has given rise to Western aphorisms about the "unchanging East"; for while it is true that Asia has seen great developments or mutations in religious and philosophic thought, great movements in art, great advances in knowledge and great vicissitudes in the fortunes of peoples and nations, there has been throughout recorded history until very recent times but little change in the fundamental social and political habits prevailing in Asiatic countries. The life of the peasant, his attitude to his rulers and their attitude to him, remained in the early nineteenth century, and in some parts of Asia still remain today, what they were in the days of Confucius in China or the Buddha in India.

The European scene is livelier. Onward from the days of the Aegean city-states it continues to manifest the restless energy which impelled Hellenic culture to expand, to reach out to other lands and peoples. There are dark and silent intervals, and sometimes the Hellenic spirit seems to be in danger of extinction; but it reasserts itself and continues to exert upon the Eastern as well as the Western world an influence which cannot be permanently resisted.

•   •   •

In studying the earliest recorded intercourse between Europe and Asia one is struck by a contrast between the strong interest in Asia displayed by European peoples and the indifference of settled Asiatic peoples to the affairs and customs of the inhabitants of distant regions. The Chinese, though inveterate chroniclers, have always affected to regard the outer world as barbaric. Their dynastic histories and even their great books of travel seem usually to state facts about foreign countries with a dry reserve. They are interested but not excited by the outside world. As for India, it is remarkable that, despite a long history of relationships with peoples beyond her northwestern frontiers, beginning with a prehistoric affinity between Hindus and Persians and continuing down to close cultural contacts with Greeks and men of Greek descent, there is in Indian literature or tradition nothing about Europe or even western Asia to compare with the copious information about India which is furnished by early Greek and Latin authors. Indeed, so little, it would seem, did the sages and scholars of India concern themselves with examining the nature of the visible world of matter, so immersed were they in speculation upon loftier themes, that the modern student must rely for much of his knowledge of ancient India upon the notices of Herodotus, Strabo, Pliny, and other classical historians and geographers who drew upon European sources of direct observation, such as Megasthenes and Ctesias. He can depend but little upon direct description in native Indian literature, since most of the information on political and social matters derived from that source is built up by inference out of religious and ethical writings or epic poems. These, while they are wanting in important historical details, testify to a rich and complex civilization evolving from its own original elements and little subject to influence from outside. "Where such influence might be looked for with greatest certainty," says an authority, "namely in the effect of Greek domination, it is practically nil. Only the Yavanas or Yonas—the "Ionians," peoples of Greek descent—who appear in Indian records from the third century B.C. to the second century A.D., remain to show that Alexander and subsequent Greek invaders left any trace. "Political and social relations do not appear to be affected at all either by Hellenic or Persian influence. . . . The social theory remains practically the same, save that a place among degraded 'outcastes' is given to Yavanas as to other barbarians." It is significant that, of all the Greek or Graeco-Indian princes who ruled either north or south of the Hindu Kush, only one is celebrated in the ancient literature of India. This is Menander, who figures in Buddhist legend not as a powerful monarch— which indeed he was—but as a philosopher who was overcome in debate and at length converted by an Indian sage. Similarly a later foreign ruler, Kanishka, appears in Indian chronicles not as a sovereign who made the Kushana empire paramount in northern India but rather as a great patron of Buddhism, second only to Asoka.

From these and many similar indications, one must conclude that Indian culture, by the time that Greek influence was brought to bear upon it, was already so deeply rooted as to be no longer open to change. The position is clearly described by an authority on the Greek, Scythian, and Parthian invasions of India, in the following words: "In Bactria the Greeks ruled supreme amid peoples of a lower culture. On the south of the mountain barrier, in the Kabul valley and in India, they were brought into contact with a civilization which was in many respects as advanced as their own and even more ancient—a civilization in which religious and social institutions had long ago been stereotyped and in which individual effort in literature and art was no longer free but bound by centuries of tradition."

Turning to China, we see a picture of relationships between East and West which, although it presents some special features due to the remoter situation of China and the distinct character of its people, does in its essentials resemble that of the intercourse between Europe and India. There is fairly abundant material in Greek and Latin works, as well as in Chinese records, giving accounts of commercial and diplomatic exchanges between China and the West in classical times. Much of it is obscure, but there is sufficient evidence to show the general character of this intercourse and its extent. We need not concern ourselves with the earliest indications of Western knowledge of China, which are of uncertain value; but for the closing years of the second century B.C. there is good documentary proof of relations between China and the western parts of Asia in which people of European stock resided. This came about through Chinese initiative. It was, however, the result not of a desire for intercourse on a footing of equality but of a search for possible allies in China's struggle against the Huns (Hiung-nu) who were then threatening her northwestern borders.

England and Japan

One of the most exciting periods in Japanese life is, to my mind, the end of the Sengoku period, where it merges into the period we may call Adzuchi-Momoyama. It appears to have had a heroic and boisterous quality which gradually vanished as the country settled down to peace. It had that gusto which is often described as the chief characteristic of the Elizabethan age in England. Let me try to say in a few words what that "gusto" means. I suppose it means first of all a strong taste, little delicacy, little refinement but a great appetite for life, lived not with miserly precautions, but in a spendthrift fashion. This, in England, was a great age of experiment and adventure, and its character is revealed as much by its literature as in its historical records. It was a violent age, a cruel age, in many ways a coarse and vulgar age, but it had for a

Sir George B. Sansom, *Japan in World History* (London: George Allen & Unwin Ltd., 1952), pp. 46-53. Reprinted by permission of the publisher.

generation or so all the engaging qualities of high-spirited youth facing the world with hope and courage, with untroubled confidence and unalloyed zest. All this you can find in Shakespeare's plays, but also in the modest prose of common men in letters, diaries, pamphlets, and scraps of recorded speech in the farm, the townsman's house and the tavern. This was the day of soldiers who were poets, and poets who were diplomats, and admirals who were historians, and explorers who were both pirates and puritans. You have only to think of such names as Sidney, Milton, Raleigh, Drake, Hawkins, to see how this age could combine artistic genius with splendid achievement in practical affairs. And how strong is the contrast with this modern introspective age, when we are sure of nothing, but full of misgivings about our physical and moral health!

I find in the Japan of Nobunaga and Hideyoshi the same kind of quality that distinguishes the Elizabethan era. The resemblances are, I think, striking. You get the end of a feudal regime and a striving to refashion society. New men come into power, and new horizons are opened to Japan, not, it is true, by discovery but by being discovered. There is a sense of adventure in the air, and bold designs are born in the minds of men who in the previous era would have remained obscure. They are spacious days.

While they last, Japanese sea-rovers are trading and fighting all over the Far East. Everything is on a grand scale—not only battles but buildings and decoration. There is a great mingling of classes, there are monster entertainments like Hideyoshi's Tea Party. There are ambitious designs like those of Nobunaga and Hideyoshi for the conquest of China. In religion there is a strong attack on the power of the Buddhist church, and altogether one gains the impression from the history of this period that Japan was about to enter upon a phase of rapid expansion and diversity in her national life and of far-ranging activity in eastern Asia, and beyond.

I do not know how full a record of everyday life has been preserved in diaries, letters and other forms, and I suppose that this period is perhaps not so rich in literary remains as contemporary England; but I would like to see the culture of Adzuchi and Momoyama described by a social historian not in a mere chronicle of events but in a study of the daily lives of soldiers and peasants, of painters and poets, so that we could at least glimpse the color and movement of this brief period which—as I have suggested—bears so many resemblances to the rough, vigorous, expansive days of Queen Elizabeth. One sad point of likeness is that both periods soon lost the bloom of youth. That also calls for explanation.

But in the search for resemblances one must be careful not to neglect differences, and there are some important differences in this case. Throughout the sixteenth century Japan was in a state of endemic civil war, whereas under Elizabeth, England enjoyed a substantial unity. That unity, the fruit of past history, was preserved by the feeling of common danger under the menace of continental powers, so that the rulers of England were free from the embarrassments of civil strife and were able without much difficulty to maintain sufficient order within the realm. The main interests of the English people at that time were defense against aggression from the European continent, and concurrently the expansion of foreign trade. But Nobunaga and Hideyoshi, though they both had ambitious visions of overseas expansion, were chiefly concerned with the political unification of their own country, and other designs had to wait on its accomplishment. Consequently, Nobunaga and particularly Hideyoshi felt obliged to put their greatest effort into subduing the great unreconciled feudatories, building up a central power, and reinforcing a rigid feudal discipline, even more rigid than that of the Minamoto and the Hojo regimes.

In England, the case was different, for when the last feudal revolts were suppressed—and feudalism was already in decay before Elizabeth's time—there was no possibility of a revival of feudal institutions. The merchants, the small farmers, the small traders, and the land-owning gentry were too powerful to be regimented. There was a wide distribution of property which made money count as much as birth, so that class barriers were lowered and the disorderly individualist temper of the day would not have tolerated any reimposition of feudal discipline.

How was it that Nobunaga and Hideyoshi were able without much difficulty to impose upon the Japanese people a discipline more severe and to enforce a class system more rigid than ever before? How does one explain the success of Hideyoshi's Sword Hunt? I suppose the reasons are various; and one, no doubt, was the long military tradition of strict feudal rule. But I should say that the most important was the preponderance of agriculture and the relatively small size and influence of the mercantile and industrial element in the population. Japan's foreign trade was never until the nineteenth century more than a trickle. It was composed largely of articles of luxury and did not bring to Japan many useful commodities which would serve the expansion of her economy.

There were plenty of skilful traders in Japan, and there was no lack of an adventurous spirit. The merchants of Sakai for a brief space enjoyed a large measure of independence and influence not unlike that of the free cities of Europe. But they were not strong enough to resist the power of feudal rulers, and though they flourished in Ashikaga times and lent money to the Shoguns, they were before long shorn of their privileges. Nobunaga and Hideyoshi and later Ieyasu were aware of the value of foreign trade in a very general way, and took some steps to encourage it. But trade promotion was not a cardinal point in their policy, and where there was a conflict of interests as between the mainte-nance of autocracy and the furtherance of trade, it was trade that had to suffer. It is scarcely possible to exaggerate the importance of this feature in Japanese history, and indeed of Chinese history also. Think, by contrast, of the importance of trade in European history, and look for example at the case of England in that Elizabethan age of which I have been speaking.

I live in a part of England which was the home of the woollen industry five hundred years ago. Not far from us are villages with such names as Jersey, Linsey, or Worsted, which gave their names to woollen cloths manufactured by local guilds and sent by mer-chants as far afield as Novgorod in Russia and Aleppo in Syria. These were the beginnings of English capitalism and of modern international trade; and today we see around us in the now quiet countryside the great churches and the fine houses built with the wealth acquired from the export of our textiles. The Crown and the Government were obliged to pay attention to foreign trade, to legislate for its improvement and control. Trade was a matter of the highest importance in the State, and fifteenth-century pol-itics were much concerned with matters arising from the com-petition of foreign trading companies. By the end of the fifteenth century—indeed well before the year 1500—it was a common-place in English thought and a maxim of English policy that England's strength—one might say, her survival—depended upon her seaborne trade. Behind all the romantic exploits of the Eliza-bethans, the voyages, peaceful or piratical, the clashes of diplo-macy and the wars on land and sea, was a constant urge to find new international markets, to discover what was called a "vent" for English exports. No wonder that poetry and prose were written in favor of trade, and even an era of international peace was predicted, to arise out of the benefits of international commerce. A typical instance is that of Pope's long poem *Windsor Forest,* written about 1712, in which he says:

> The time shall come when free as seas or wind
> Unbounded Thames shall flow for all mankind,
> Whole nations enter with each swelling tide
> And seas but join the regions they divide.
>
> . . .
>
> O stretch thy reign, fair Peace! from shore to shore,
> Till conquest cease and slavery be no more.

Another English poet, John Dyer, wrote in 1757 an excessively long poem (almost an epic) called *The Fleece,* which is devoted to sheep-farming, the treatment of wool, the manufacture of woollen cloth and its sale throughout the world. In his concluding stanzas he predicts that England will clothe the world "from Anian's straits to proud Japan."

Compare this preoccupation with commerce to the attitude of the Tokugawa rulers. Nobunaga and Hideyoshi had up to a point encouraged foreign trade, because they perceived some of its benefits and indeed themselves profited by it. Ieyasu was also loth to forgo the advantages of commerce. He was prepared to negotiate with foreign countries and desired to build good ocean-going ships. But none of these rulers regarded trade as the life-blood of the state, and nothing in past history had taught them that Japan could not indefinitely maintain a self-sufficient economy. That lesson was learned by the small maritime countries of Europe because they were poor and weak by comparison with the great land-powers. Japan, on the other hand, had no such experience, and did not feel impelled to risk the dangers of international intercourse. Consequently she remained substantially an agrarian state, though with a remarkably developed domestic trade and industry; and thus the merchant class, which steadily gained power in England, was checked and thwarted in Japan and denied political power until after the Restoration of 1868.

IV / SOCIAL STRUCTURE

One can distill a "spirit" from the way things seem to be in history. But this is not to say that the spirit *accounts* for the things. As a matter of fact, one should be wary of speaking of "the Chinese spirit," say, as distinct from the spirit of these Chinese or those. It is a cardinal historical error to interpret an idea, attitude, or "spirit" that is the product of historical development as the *ground* of historical development. Although the Chinese rejected Mo Tzu, a philosopher who lived in the generation after Confucius, it was not because Mo Tzu flouted "the perennial Chinese values" of reasonableness, harmony, and moderation. Although Buddhism was ultimately worn down in China, it was not because "the Chinese mind is normally" practical, skeptical, and this-worldly. These nouns and these adjectives, however applicable they may be to a long stretch of history, do not constitute an inherent spirit of the Chinese people.

If these characteristics constitute a spirit at all, it is rather the reflection of Confucian civilization, which was a historical, explicable experience; the spirit is not a natural endowment, to be simply accepted as given. Confucian civilization, long-lived but not eternal, was not there at the beginning of Chinese history. It had its own beginnings, in the middle and late first millennium B.C., perhaps a thousand years after the continuities of what may be called Chinese civilization were established. And the experience of the nineteenth and twentieth centuries suggest that it could have an end.

This brings us back to Ming China (1368-1644), a conservative China, surely, as Confucianism is conservative. But a conservative spirit is what we deduce from the operations of Ming society, which encompassed a "Western" potential for far-reaching commerce and navigation, but rendered it abortive.

The following selection, describing Chinese commerce in Southeast Asia before 1500, reflects the extent of this potential that was never realized, indicating that Chinese trade and settlement existed in Southeast Asia, precisely where the Portuguese and the Dutch and the English were to take the play away from the Chinese.

15 / CHINESE "EXPANSION"

One is struck by the significant part played by the Chinese in the [East Indies] archipelago in the fourteenth century. The Malay-Indonesian area was a resting place for Chinese en route to the West—probably Chinese established themselves there permanently in Çrivijaya's [Java] heyday. In this connection, Coedès draws attention to a remark made by the Moslem writer Edrisi in 1154, stating that when revolts led to very disturbed conditions in China some of the people of that country transferred their trade to Zabag (Çrivijaya) and its dependent territories and entered into business relations with the local inhabitants. The land of San-fo-ts'i, as Çrivijaya is called in Chinese sources, must have been well known to the Chinese because of Çrivijaya's many business connections with China. And when Çrivijaya degenerated into the pirate stronghold of Palembang the pirates themselves were Chinese.

Peaceable Chinese merchants used to visit the pepper port of Pase, possibly even before the rise of Malacca. Ibn Battuta mentions that gold ingots from China were in circulation there alongside the native coins of tin, and his description of the way the native houses were furnished is also indicative of Chinese influence.

Relations of very long standing also existed between China and Java, as the many archeological finds of Chinese earthenware and coins indicate. Javanese missions visited the Imperial Court with the tribute which China claimed from the southern "barbarians," and Chinese merchants and colonists went to Indonesia from China in search of pepper and valuable kinds of wood. A punitive ex-

From M. A. P. Meilink-Roelofsz, *Asian Trade and European Influence in the Indonesian Archipelago Between 1500 and About 1630* (The Hague: Martinus Nijhoff, 1962), pp. 25-6. Reprinted by permission of the publisher. Footnotes omitted.

pedition which China undertook against East Java at the end of the thirteenth century had not affected commercial relations.

To the towns of Java the Chinese brought porcelain, silken materials and yarns, musk, gold, silver, iron, beads, and vast quantities of their small copper coins, by means of which they conducted a lucrative trade with the Javanese. Numerous Chinese settled in Java where they helped to found the Javanese seaports and stimulated their growth to such an extent that the foundation of a port like Grise, for example, is attributed in Chinese sources to Chinese enterprise.

Since the Javanese ports lay on the Chinese route to the Spice Islands, and since the coveted spices could be obtained in these ports in profusion, it is probable that the Chinese went to Timor for sandalwood but seldom visited the actual Spice Islands. Confirmation of this theory may be found in the fact that these islands receive only very sporadic mention in Chinese sources.

When, however, a new commercial center, Malacca, came into existence on the Malay Straits, the Chinese must have reduced their trade with the Javanese ports considerably, at least that would seem to be the implication of Pires' remark that in his day (circa 1515) Chinese merchants had not been seen in the Javanese ports for the past 100 years. But although the Chinese shipping trade to Java was reduced in volume, Chinese establishments in the towns continued to exist and the Chinese continued to have a large share in Javanese trade.

16 / THE CHINESE EMPEROR VERSUS THE BUREAUCRACY

What was it that damaged China's dynamic possibilities for expansion? Throughout Confucian-imperial history, there is evidence to indicate that the imperial institution (though a formidable monopolist and dispenser of monopolies) did not essentially restrain trade as a way of life. But the Confucian bureaucracy did. Bureaucrats profited from trade, but they profited as parasites, draining what provided part of their wealth. This distinction between monarch and Confucian official (who nevertheless needed each other) was only one of many that made Confucian China a world held in equilibrium by a stabilizing tension between the two institutions of monarchy and bureaucracy, each depending on the other, each restraining the other (see Joseph R. Levenson, Confucian China and Its Modern Fate, Volume II; The Problem of Monarchical Decay).

Note, in the first of the following selections, an imperial decision in favor of freeing trade; and, in the next three selections, the Confucian drag on imperial initiative. When our friend, the naval hero, Cheng Ho returns, we must keep in mind that he was an outsider to the Confucianists: a Muslim and (of supreme significance) a eunuch. For all through Chinese imperial history, eunuchs were drawn (though their influence fluctuated from dynasty to dynasty and even within dynastic reigns) into coteries of king's-men, dependent on (though sometimes overshadowing) the monarchs who unmade them. They formed useful rival coteries to the monarchs' ambivalent servants, the socially and intellectually prestigious corps of literati-officials.

An Imperial Liberal Decision on Foreign Trade

. . . The emperor commented on the . . . arrival of Muslim traders from Siam. The comment reads as follows:

> Lately the Muslim Haji and others from the "Western Ocean" were at Siam when our mission arrived and they followed the mission back to the court. Such distant foreigners who know respect for China are indeed praiseworthy. Now that they are being sent home, the Ministry of Rites should give them the credentials to ensure that the officials on their way will not obstruct them. From now on all foreign nations who wish to come to China may be allowed to do so.

This was followed three weeks later (14 November) by the emperor's refusal to tax Muslim traders for selling pepper. The entry in the *Yung-lo Shih-lu* reads:

> The Muslim Haji Ma-ha-mo Ch'i-ni and others from the country of Hsi-yang La-ni [?] came to the court with a tribute of native goods. Because they traded the pepper which they brought with the people, the authorities asked that this trade be taxed. The emperor replied, "The commercial tax is for the purpose of discouraging people from pursuing trade as a profession and surely not for profit to the state. Now the foreigners have come from afar out of admiration for us and we want to cut into his profits. We can only get very little [revenue] while this will completely degrade our principles." The request was rejected.

From Wang Gungwu, "The Opening of Relations Between China and Malacca, 1403-5," in John Bastin and R. Roolvink, eds., *Malayan and Indonesian Studies: Essays presented to Sir Richard Winstedt on his eighty-fifth birthday* (Oxford: Clarendon Press, 1964), p. 94. Reprinted by permission of the publisher. Footnotes omitted.

Confucian-Bureaucratic Inhibition of Foreign Trade

The emperor who declined to permit "the authorities" (Confucian officials) to harass the Muslim traders was the same emperor (Yung-lo, one of the strongest in Chinese history) who authorized Cheng Ho's expeditions. But the Confucianists had more staying power than individual emperors, and Confucian social values set the ultimately prevailing tone.

The Moral Reproach to Cheng Ho

The beginning of the Ming dynasty saw an unparalled effort on the part of the Chinese government to reopen the foreign trade.

During the long interlude when the Mongols dominated all Asia, the intercourse between East and West had been very lively, but with the downfall of the Mongols and the breakup of their vast Empire, the trade-routes became blocked and the imports to which the Chinese had become used ceased to flow. In the Chinese conception of the importance of foreign trade there were always mixed considerations. From a practical point of view, foreign trade meant prosperity to countless numbers of people who profited from it; the Treasury was swelled by the import-duties, and although, as we have seen, the outflow of cash was an evil, the advantages of foreign trade, particularly to the southern provinces, were considerable. Now all overseas commerce had chiefly to do with articles of luxury: all kinds of precious stones, fragrant woods, spices, rare objects, and the consumers of these goods were the wealthy classes, first and foremost the Court and its harem ladies. Ideologically, however, this state of affairs was never admitted: in the Confucian theory trade was regarded as something inferior, almost sordid, with which as such the Emperor could never have anything to do. Therefore the form in which relations with overseas nations are always represented is that of tribute-bearing. The barbarians came from afar, recognizing the overlordship of the Son of Heaven and bringing tribute, after which they were graciously allowed to trade. In the past Chinese envoys had repeatedly been dispatched overseas to induce foreign nations to come to China to bring tribute, thus increasing both the prestige of the Chinese Emperor and their own. The more foreign envoys present at the New Year's audiences at Court the more illustrious was the glory of the Emperor, who

From J. J. L. Duyvendak, *China's Discovery of Africa* (London: Arthur Probsthain, 1949), pp. 26-8. Reprinted by permission of the publisher. Footnotes omitted.

like the Duke of Chou of old, succeeded by his sage government in attracting foreign barbarians.

These mixed motives: the real need of overseas products felt particularly at Court, and the desire to increase his own prestige and re-establish the overseas renown of the Chinese Empire, must have prompted the third Emperor of the Ming dynasty to undertake a series of missions overseas. In the official Annals still another motive is adduced, namely, a political one. The Yung-lo Emperor, son of the founder, only gained the throne by deposing his young nephew, to whom the throne had been bequeathed. The nephew disappeared: it was rumored that he had fled overseas, and therefore a fleet was sent out to try and bring him back from the countries of the barbarians, where he was supposed to be hiding. The excuse is transparent; for such a purpose it would not have been necessary to undertake expeditions on such scale as sailed, not merely once, but at least seven times, not counting minor ones. Some of them comprised no less than sixty-two vessels, carrying 37,000 soldiers; more than thirty countries in the Indian archipelago and the Indian Ocean were visited, and besides ports in the Persian Gulf, places like Aden and Mecca were visited and the Chinese ships sailed all the way to Africa.

The most extraordinary thing is that these fleets were placed under the command of a Court eunuch, Cheng Ho, a Mohammedan, the son of Hadji Ma, from Yunnan, with whom several other eunuchs, as well as military officers were associated. He is popularly known as San-pao-t'ta-chien, . . . "the Three-jewel Eunuch," and the ships under his command were designated as pao-ch'uan, "jewel-ships.". . .

Now, if we remember that already from the days of Wu-ti on in the second century B.C., eunuchs were sent on such overseas expeditions, we see a striking example of that extraordinary continuity of Chinese institutions which makes it possible to illustrate and explain a given historical fact by something that happened a thousand years earlier or later. Just as was the case with those early eunuchs, Cheng Ho was put in command of these expeditions because he had to purvey articles of luxury for the Court; if I may say so, he went ashopping for the ladies of the Imperial harem.

The sources for our knowledge of these expeditions are varied and there has been much confusion. The official reports of Cheng Ho's voyages are no longer extant. How is this to be explained, when it is certain that he must have presented long memorials about his voyages and so much other documentary material has been preserved? This is directly connected with the fact that he was a eunuch. While the expeditions into Central Asia by various generals, under Wu-ti, are part of the nation's historical tradition, as something redounding to China's credit, Cheng Ho's expeditions, equally remarkable in themselves, have been almost completely forgotten. It is said that about 1480 another eunuch who had risen to great power, wished to imitate Cheng Ho and start a maritime expedition against Annam. For this purpose he asked for the official records of Cheng Ho's expeditions. With the connivance of the high officials of the War Office these records were thereupon destroyed, so as to frustrate the eunuch's attempts to organize an expedition. There was, during the Ming dynasty, a strong rivalry between the official classes and the eunuchs, who were privately employed by the Emperor in various important functions. This was very galling to the official classes who, anyway, as good Confucianists, despised trade and luxury and looked down upon foreign barbarians. The entire business of relations with overseas barbarians became, in the moral and political judgment of the official classes, inextricably bound up with their deep sense of disapproval of the extravagances and usurpation of power of the despised eunuchs. This feeling was not even relieved by the sense of gratification at the homage paid to the Chinese Emperor by so many distant countries, to which was added the fact that the expeditions were expensive and unprofitable. To them China, being economically sufficient unto itself, could very well do without the products of foreign countries which were nothing but curiosities. This deep-rooted aversion contributed to the formation of that peculiar Confucianistic mentality of the ruling classes that later, when Western nations came to trade, caused so much difficulty. These after-effects of Cheng Ho's voyages should, therefore, not be overlooked by the students of China's modern history.

The Suppression of the Records of the Ming Voyages

It is a very curious thing that the maritime expeditions which so greatly enhanced China's prestige throughout the Eastern world and which, while they flattered the Emperor's pride, at the same time established trade relations with overseas countries as never before, ceased as completely as they did. They took place less than a century before the Portuguese advent in Far Eastern waters. If

From J. J. L. Duyvendak, "The True Dates of the Chinese Maritime Expeditions in the Early Fifteenth Century," *T'oung Pao*, Vol. 34, Book 5 (1939), pp. 395-99. Reprinted by permission of E. J. Brill Ltd., Leiden. Footnotes omitted.

China had continued Yung-lo's policy of encouraging foreign trade and overseas relations, the course of history might have been different. But not only did the expeditions completely end, even their memory scarcely seems to have continued. The references to Cheng Ho's voyages are scarce and extremely superficial; at no time do they seem to have been part of the picture of a "glorious past." The accounts of the journeys of Ma Huan, Fei Hsin, and Kung Chen were never widely spread, and the notices in other books are scattered and difficult of access. Cheng Ho's biography in the *Ming-shih* is the only coherent account that may have come under the eyes of the average scholar. But how is it that no official reports of these voyages seem to have been preserved? Surely Cheng Ho and his associates must have presented complete accounts of their voyages to the Emperor.

The answer to this question is of great interest. The story that is told, though at first glance it sounds rather fantastic, is far less so on second thought.

Ku Ch'i-yüan writes in his *K'o-tso Chui-yu,* . . . ch. 1, p. 30*a* that in the Ch'eng-hua period (1465-1487) an order was given to search for the documents concerning the expeditions to the Western Ocean which were kept in the War Office. Liu Ta-hsia . . . , who then was Vice-president of the Board, having taken them, burnt them, being of opinion that their contents were

> deceitful exaggerations of bizarre things far removed from the testimony of people's ears and eyes. The local products which they contributed were nothing but betel . . . , *ch'iung-chang* . . . [bamboo staves], grape-vine . . . , pomegranates . . . [*cf.* H. Laufer, *Sino-Iranica,* pp. 278, 282], and large birds' eggs [ostrich eggs] and such like odd things. The account of the *Hsing-ch'a-sheng-lan* is rare and cannot be examined.

In ch. 8 of the *Shu-yu Chou-tzu-lu,* which, it should be remembered, is the product of the Hsing-jen-ssu, to whose special office pertained all relations with foreigners, the same story with additions is repeated. It reports (ch. 8, p. 26*b*) that an order was issued by the Emperor to search out the itinerary of Cheng Ho's expeditions, and that the President of the War Office, Hsiang Chung . . . , instructed an official to go into the archives to search for the old documents but that they could not be found. For indeed, they had previously been hidden by the *Chu-chia Lang-chung* (Vice-president) Liu Ta-hsia. Hsiang Chung had the official beaten and again caused him to search for three days but in the end nothing could be found. Liu Ta-hsia kept his action secret. . . .

Hsiang Chung questioned the officials saying: "How is it possible that official documents in the archives are lost?" Liu Ta-hsia, standing on one side, remarked:

> The expeditions of the San-pao to the Western Ocean wasted tens of myriads of money and grain, and moreover the people who met their deaths [on these expeditions] may be counted by the myriads. Although he returned with wonderful precious things, what benefit was it to the state? This was merely an action of bad government of which ministers should severely disapprove. Even if the old archives were still preserved they should be destroyed in order to suppress [a repetition of these things] at the root.

Hsiang Chung listened quietly, rose from his seat and said: "Your hidden virtue, Sir, is not small; surely this seat will shortly be yours!"

A study of the biographies in the *Ming-shih* (in ch. 178 and ch. 182) of the two men named considerably clarifies the situation and confirms the essentials of the story. What they did, was to oppose the power of the eunuch Wang Chih . . . , who in the Ch'eng-hua period was extremely influential. In 1479 he was appointed Inspector of the Frontiers and in connection with troubles about Annam, he was planning an expedition into that country. For that purpose he desired to see the records of Yung-lo's time.

Not having the power to stop Wang Chih's ambitious schemes, the high officials of the War Office must have resorted to this method of withholding from him the information that might have encouraged his plans. Liu Ta-hsia, who later rose to high office and eventually became indeed Minister of War, entirely had the ear of his chief, and could scarcely have acted as he did without being sure of the latter's tacit approval.

In this light the story does not seem so improbable. During the Ming dynasty a secret war was waged by the officials against the encroachments of their power by the eunuchs. The fact that eunuchs filled such high positions, led important expeditions, and were at the head of large armies must have profoundly irritated them. The prospect of a powerful eunuch like Wang Chih wishing to take a leaf out of Cheng Ho's book was to them extremely distasteful and they therefore resorted to the stratagem of hiding or destroying the documents. So the real reason why the memory of Cheng Ho's expeditions almost vanished from the records is to be sought in the fact that they were the deeds of a eunuch. The entire business of relations with overseas barbarians became, in the moral and political judgment of Chinese scholars and officials, inextricably bound up with their sense of disapproval of the extravagances and usurpation of power by the despised eunuchs. Even the sense of gratification at the homage paid to the Chinese Emperor by so many distant countries was repressed by this deep-rooted feeling of disapproval. Added to this was the consciousness that the expeditions were very expensive and unprofitable, as had already been pointed out during Yung-lo's lifetime. The strength of the opposition even then may be gauged from the fact that, as narrated before, the first act of Yung-lo's successor was to lift this extra burden from the shoulders of the people. Though Chinese officialdom was never concerned about the welfare of the people when their own position was in question, the argument came in very profitably when the real objection was to the power laid in the hands of their great rivals, the eunuchs. This aversion helps to explain why in later times such expeditions have never been repeated. It also contributed to the formation of the Confucian mentality which frustrated fruitful intercourse with overseas barbarians in modern times. The desire for closer intercourse was felt to be unworthy of a Confucian official; such a desire was identified with luxury and eunuch rule, it was extravagant and wasteful, and China, being economically sufficient unto herself, could very well do without the curiosities produced by foreign countries. The expeditions of Cheng Ho had, geographically, furnished all the knowledge that was necessary or useful; the barbarians and their customs had become sufficiently well known; further contact was decidedly not to be desired. . . .

The Abortiveness of the Ming Initiative

The question may be asked, what were the practical results of these amazing expeditions [of Cheng Ho], in which hundreds of ocean-going junks and several tens of thousands of men were used? The short answer would be, absolutely none. The Ming Chinese were not empire-builders. Their political pundits had no conception of the horrors of *realpolitik* inseparable from a colonial regime. They had no sense of mission, no idea of *sturm und drang*. Theoretically the Son of Heaven ruled the whole world, *t'ien hsia'*, "all under heaven," and his envoys considered it enough to show themselves around, to display themselves to the nondescript bar-

From William Willetts, "The Maritime Adventures of Grand Eunuch Ho," in Colin Jack-Hinton, ed., *Papers on Early South-east Asian History* (Singapore: The Journal of Southeast Asian History, 1964), pp. 30-31, 36-8. Reprinted by permission of the publishers. Footnotes omitted.

barians on the fringes of the civilized world, in order to usher in a millennium activated by the serene presence of the Son of Heaven upon the Throne. In effect, therefore, they accomplished nothing durable. . . .

· · ·

Earlier . . . it was remarked that the incredible flotillas sent across the seas by the Yung-lo Emperor were barren of any practical outcome, but this was not in fact strictly the case. After Cheng Ho's farewell voyage of 1431-33 no fresh naval excursion was launched by China, and the barbarians of the Western Ocean soon began to realize that they need no longer continue to send their tribute-gifts to Peking. The stream of "ambassadors" became a trickle, and then dried completely. Ceylon, for instance, sent an embassy in 1445 led by one Ya-pa-la-mo-ti-li-ya (Jayapala Mudaliya), and fourteen years later a second followed. But thereafter, as *Ming shih* notes: "no further tribute reached China from that quarter." Another fifty years, and the Portuguese would arrive and lash the Indian seas into a new turmoil; but for the moment there was peace and quiet.

Why did not the Chinese follow up the tremendous initial advantage they had gained as a result of Cheng Ho's ventures? The answer, as given by Professor Duyvendak, is a curious one, yet throws light on an enigma whose meaning has always eluded foreign observers of the Chinese—that official xenophobia which, over the centuries, has characterized China's diplomatic dealings with the rest of the world, and indeed has conditioned her response to the whole question of foreigners and foreign contacts.

We can date with some exactness the onset of this strange malady, soon to become chronic. When Yung-lo's successor, the Hsuan-tsang Emperor, gave his sanction to Cheng Ho's voyage of 1431-33 he obviously did so against the opposition of many of his ministers, and for that matter against his own better judgment. For on the very day he came to the Throne, September 7th, 1424, he had issued the following order: "The ships for fetching precious stones which go to the barbarian countries of the Western Ocean are all stopped. If there are any that are already anchored in Fuchien . . . they should all return to Nanking. The building of seaships for going to the barbarian [countries] should everywhere be stopped." The Emperor took this measure on the advice of one who had already years earlier memorialized the Yung-lo Emperor to the effect that "eunuchs were building large ships to enter into communication with overseas countries," leaving him to draw his own conclusions as to where that sort of thing would lead.

We have here in fact an expression of the pathological hatred felt by Confucian officialdom towards the eunuchs, a hatred that can be traced back in Chinese history for the best part of two thousand years. Over much of that history, it is true, the eunuch was indeed a grossly unedifying specimen, with his infinite capacity for dirty intrigue in the Inner Court, and his unpleasant habit of paying others to do his political murders for him. But at the period with which we are concerned, eunuchs were no hothouse plants of weedy and invertebrate growth, but hardy perennials that throve out-of-doors, under blinding suns and racing storm clouds. Cheng Ho was by no means the only eunuch on the high seas at the beginning of Ming times. On the 1431 voyage, as we read in the inscription on the T'ai-p'ing Bay stone, he was accompanied by Wang Ching-hung, Li Hsing, Chu Liang, Chou Man, Hung Pao, Yang Chen, Chang Ta, Wu Chung, all Grand Eunuchs, and the naval commanders Chu Chen and Wang Heng, not to mention the interpreter Ma Huan. Many of these men had been on independent missions; Hung Pao and Chou Man, for instance, had been almost entirely responsible for the sixth expedition of 1421, and the expedition to Bengal 1412-24 was led by another of the fellowship called Yang Ch'in or Yang Min. It is obvious that men like these were not to be trifled with.

The conservative Confucianists, however, regarded the whole crew with utter loathing. You could in any case hardly call them men; and, since they were all sunk in the squalor of some foreign superstitions, you could hardly call them Chinese either. They were of course plotting for power, and it was absolutely vital to put a stop to their activities.

17 / PAPER CURRENCY IN CHINA

The same Ming dynasty that saw Chinese navigation reach out and then pull back inherited another "modern" economic feature from the Mongol conquest-dynasty of Yüan, 1279-1368—and relinquished it as well: paper currency. Again the Ming seemed to have the modern world in their grasp, then loosened their grip. The next selection describes the career of paper money in China.

From Lien-sheng Yang, *Money and Credit in China: A Short History* (Cambridge: Harvard University Press, 1952), pp. 64-8. © 1952 by the Harvard-Yenching Institute. Reprinted by permission of the publisher.

The Yuan dynasty marks the climax in the evolution of early Chinese paper money. The origins of Yuan paper currency lie directly in the systems of Sung and Chin, but eventually developed far beyond them. After the Yuan, paper money declined rapidly and practically disappeared after the sixteenth century. The revival of paper currency in the nineteenth century was largely the result of the impact of economic forces from the Western world.

. . .

In its heyday, the Yuan paper currency circulated not only in Chinese and Uighur areas but also penetrated to Burma, Siam, and Annam. It was also introduced into Persia, where the Mongols ruled for many years. There paper money was known as *cau* from the Chinese *ch'ao* and reckoned in *balis*, "pillow," similar to a *ting*. Together with paper notes, Chinese banking practices became known to the West. Max Weber states that the accounting system (*Verrechnungswesen*) of the old Hamburg Bank was set up on a Chinese model. Robert Eisler suggests that the old Swedish system of banking and money deposit vouchers may have been influenced by Chinese examples, transmitted by medieval merchant-travelers and, possibly, by Jewish silk merchants.

. . .

A few years after the reunification of China by the Ming dynasty, its founder, T'ai-tsu, attempted a revival of paper currency. In 1374 a *Pao-ch'ao t'i-chu-ssu,* or "Precious Note Control Bureau," was established and in the following year a note called *Ta-Ming pao-ch'ao,* "Precious Note of the Great Ming," was issued. T'ai-tsu's reign title, Hung-wu, appeared on the note. In honor of the founder of the dynasty, notes printed in later reigns also bore the same reign title, although the other Ming emperors had their own reign titles.

From the very beginning the Ming note was inconvertible. Copper coins circulated along with paper currency, and the prohibition of the use of gold and silver as media of exchange was repeated but not enforced. The exchange value of notes declined rapidly and measures had to be taken to maintain it. In 1393 the government temporarily forbade the use of copper coins. In 1404 it decreed that a salt tax should be paid in notes in order to draw off the excess currency. In 1429 twelve regional customs stations called *ch'ao-kuan* were established to collect inland transit duties in paper currency. These devices, however, proved to be of little avail. One ounce of silver which was officially worth one string in notes in 1375, was valued at 35 strings toward the end of the fourteenth century, at 80 strings in the first quarter of the fifteenth century, and over 1000 strings by the middle of the century. Instead of paper currency, silver had become the major medium of exchange. The note practically ceased in circulation from the sixteenth century. The government only belatedly announced payments in silver for official salaries and transit duties.

The advantages of a paper currency, however, were not forgotten. This is illustrated by a proposal to revive it in the year 1643 when the dynasty was approaching its end. As many as ten advantages were listed in a memorial which pleased the Emperor greatly.

> The first was that it could be manufactured at a low cost. The second was that it could circulate widely. The third was that it could be carried with ease, being light. The fourth was that it could be readily kept in concealment. The fifth was that it was not liable to division like silver into different grades of purity. The sixth was that it did not need weighing whenever it was used in a commercial transaction as was the case with silver. The seventh advantage was that silversmiths could not clip it for their own nefarious profit. The eighth was that it was not exposed to the peering gaze of the thief's rapacity. The ninth was that if paper took the place of copper, and copper ceased to be used for making cash, there would be a saving in the cost of this metal to the government, or the copper saved could be used in manufacturing arms for the troops. The tenth advantage would be that if paper were used instead of silver, the silver might be stored up by the government.

The proposal, however, was not carried out, because the government was too weak to derive benefits from paper currency.

Silver ingots and copper cash continued to serve as the two major forms of currency in the seventeenth and eighteenth centuries. The Ch'ing dynasty, which succeeded the Ming, refrained from copying on any large scale the unworthy example of Ming notes. The only early exception was in 1650 when the government printed paper notes in the modest amount of 128,000 strings. This was an emergency measure. The same annual quota was maintained until 1661 when paper currency was abolished.

18 / THE CHINESE DIVERGENCE FROM THE PATH OF A COMMON POTENTIAL

What was the social character of this Chinese world? What enabled it to show the way to the West in proto-modern directions, and then turn away from paths the West was taking? It is the Chinese potential for expansion, already glimpsed, that makes the social blocks to the follow-through so counter-exemplary for Europe. China was not aiming at Western achievements and falling short; it was living out the values of its own quite different culture, with its different social sanctions. It was not a question of ability, but taste. Cheng Ho could sail. Paper money could circulate. But China cut them off, and the society that did it, as an inverse reflection of a new, dynamic Europe, yields some serious indications of why Europe expanded.

The next group of extracts shows a China in which the key to power was the combined possession of land and office in a tax-collecting, centralized state. The centralizer—the monarch—was not allied with anything like the European bourgeoisie, the city men, the traders with political, economic, and intellectual motives for breaking feudal fetters and surging into the world (if only by proxy). Chinese cities, for the most part, were administrative creations—certainly administration-oriented—not natural mercantile growths. Feudal aristocracy had long since been rendered insignificant. And the Chinese monarch was (ambiguously) allied with a literati-bureaucracy, certified intellectuals who had served the monarch, and served themselves, by ousting aristocracy from significant social power. Recruited through examinations, this civil bureaucracy was inherently conservative, as devoted students of ancient texts that they had to master to qualify for eminence.

The intellectual, humanistic qualifications that had set them against aristocrats (whose qualifications were military, not civil, and governed by birth, not by achievement) set them quite as conclusively against merchants and technicians. And this cultural hau-teur, manifested internally toward all the unlettered and all the grubbers for mere profit—those who were judged to be too deprived or too crude for the "higher life"—was manifested externally as well.

Social Classes in Ming

The Business Class

Mercantile and industrial groups did not pose a comparable political threat to the government [of China during the Ming dy-

From Charles O. Hucker, *The Traditional Chinese State in Ming Times* (1368-1644) (Tucson: The University of Arizona Press, 1961), pp. 30-37. Reprinted by permission of the publisher. Footnotes omitted.

nasty], but their activities were also carefully regulated. As at all times in China's past, agriculture was considered the only honorable profession except for governmental service, and profit-seeking adventurers in commerce and industry were regularly denounced by Ming rulers as being exploitive and corrupting cancers in society. Although it was recognized that they provided a service of some social utility, persons who engaged in private business ventures were consistently discriminated against in such ways as to discredit them in public esteem. They were forbidden to wear clothing of better grade silk, for example.

Merchants and industrialists customarily organized themselves into local guilds identified by the types of commodities or services with which they dealt, and the guilds largely determined the conditions of trade in their spheres. But governmental inspectors regularly checked on the accuracy of scales and measures in mercantile establishments and on the quality of goods produced in craft establishments, and they kept records of commodity prices. Anyone whose goods were of less than acceptable quantity and quality or whose prices were deemed exorbitant was subject to punishment by the government. A monthly inventory tax was collected from all businesses, and a kind of domestic customs duty was levied on all goods in transit.

Each guild had a guild chief certified by the government who was, in some measure not wholly clear, responsible to the government for the conduct of the guildsmen. Boat traders were similarly organized under harbor chiefs. Traders could travel about only with passports issued by the government, and every guild chief and harbor chief was required to present to the government each month a complete accounting of the identities and activities of all visiting traders. In order to prevent too complete monopolization of trade by resident guild chiefs, the government in some cities established its own trading warehouses, from which visiting merchants might sell directly to retail outlets.

The major factor in repressing the growth of business interests was not these supervisory restrictions on the part of government, however; it was active governmental monopolization of the production and distribution of various commodities. This monopolization had two aspects. On the one hand, manufactured goods that were consumed by the government itself were, generally speaking, produced by the government. Peking abounded with armories, textile factories, metalwork shops, leather-work shops, saddlery shops, paint shops, apparel factories, wineries, and the like, all operated by the Ministry of Works or by eunuchs, to provide the Court and the central government with their commodity needs. In addition, there were government-operated weaving and dying establishments at Nanking, Su-chou, Hang-chou, and other great cities, and a famous pottery factory at Ching-te-chen in Kiangsi province. Since the government was by far the largest single consumer of many commodities, its reliance on its own producing agencies deprived private businessmen of one of their best opportunities for enrichment.

On the other hand, the government exercised monopolistic control over the production and distribution of commodities that were essential to the population at large and susceptible to private monopolistic exploitation. Principal commodities of this type were salt and iron, which were readily available only in limited areas but were required throughout the empire. Production and distribution of these goods were directly controlled by special agencies established at appropriate places under the supervision of the central government. Each producing area was assigned a production quota and workers turned over their total product to the government. The governmental agencies in turn sold to private merchants according to quotas, and inspection stations throughout the empire seized as contraband any monopoly goods that were not accompanied by appropriate government certificates. In times of surplus, the government did not hesitate to impose impractically large quotas upon unhappy merchants. At times, too, it required merchants to earn coveted salt-purchase certificates by delivering foodstuffs to distant frontier military garrisons.

Workers in the government's industrial establishments and in the government-monopoly enterprises were generally hereditary laborers and craftsmen. Like the military families that provided sons for army service, they were considered a class apart from the general civilian population. They were organized under patriarchal foremen or masters who contracted for their services with the government and, like tithing chiefs or community chiefs, were totally responsible for their conduct. Moreover, each master was a guarantor of the good conduct of his neighboring masters.

These monopolistic and repressive tactics of the government prevented the rise of a tycoon class in Ming China. But they did not prevent the corruption of public and especially governmental morality. The evidence suggests that mercantile wealth became steadily more esteemed during the Ming period and that customs became increasingly extravagant, to the detriment of the rather puritanical agrarian values espoused by the government. Specifically, imperial clansmen, imperial in-laws, and eunuchs by the latter years of the Ming period were using their privileged positions to dabble exploitively in commercial enterprises and to corrupt the administration of state monopolies for their own benefit.

The Gentry

Of greater social significance in Ming times than either religious or business groups was the so-called gentry, a non-laboring class whose members were popularly considered persons of quality. The status was not self-perpetuating. Membership fluctuated from generation to generation in accord with the fluctuating fortunes of individual families. But the class persisted, and it monopolized local wealth and local leadership in such a way as to dominate economic and political life in the villages and towns.

From the point of view of economics, members of the gentry were landlords, money lenders, and sometimes investors in and proprietors of business establishments. To some extent they were ruthless exploiters of the peasant population. Since there was always a shortage of capital, they were able quite legally, by contract, to impose crushing rents and interest rates, and their collection agents often bullied their clients mercilessly. Recurring natural disasters enabled them to expand their holdings at the expense of bankrupt mortgagees, and poor families often delivered themselves and their properties into gentry possession, in a form of contractual serfdom, to gain protection from irregular exploitation, private or governmental. By late Ming times it was not uncommon for large gentry families to have several thousand indentured clients of this sort, some of them little more than slaves. Some gentry families came to possess little baronies, in which they extorted private tolls on travelers and on merchandise in transit.

But the gentry families were by no means completely oppressive in their economic domination of the local scene. Gentry relations with the peasantry were close and personal ones and were thus tempered with paternalistic concerns. Reliance on gentry benevolence was often the only resource available to the poor. Moreover, gentry families recognized that being persons of quality involved a certain measure of community service, and they regularly contributed schools, roads, bridges, temples, irrigation works, entertainments, charitable institutions, and other benefits to their communities.

In the political sphere gentry domination was based upon monopolization of almost all local contacts with the imperial government. It was members of the gentry who mediated between the government and the people as community chiefs and district collectors of land taxes—positions that gave their local power a semi-governmental sanction. Moreover, gentry members were the only Chinese, generally speaking, who had sufficient wealth and leisure to educate themselves, so that the gentry formed the pool of literati from which the government obtained its non-hereditary administrative personnel. The Chinese term that is traditionally rendered "gentry," as a matter of fact, literally denotes degree-holders, and the association between the local elite and government service was so close that the existence of a non-degree gentry group of large-scale landlords is questionable.

As educated men, gentry members enjoyed a camaraderie with governmental officials based on common interests, and they were the natural informants about local customs and attitudes for officials who, by rule, were never assigned to posts in their own home provinces. Gentry dominance over the local peasantry was inevitably enhanced by these social contacts with officialdom. It was further facilitated by the success of gentry sons in civil-service examinations. For one thing, status as a degree-holder automatically gave one's family important exemptions from governmental tax and *corvée* obligations, and it incidentally qualified one to augment the family's wealth by salaried service in the county governmental establishment and by earning tutorial fees. Success in the higher examinations brought possible appointments in the civil service itself, with even greater monetary returns in salaries, gifts, and irregular enhancements of income from various sources. The higher one rose in governmental service, the more his relatives back home were able to capitalize on their prestigeful connections by practicing various forms of exploitation without serious hindrance. So many opportunities for the acquisition of wealth came with degree-holding status that literati possibly begat landlords to a greater extent than landlords begat literati. Or, at least, it appears probable that constant renewal of literati privileges by examination successes generation after generation was necessary to perpetuate wealth and large-scale landownership.

The gentry was a social and economic class rather than a formally organized group in society. It was locally-based and family-oriented. Gentry families cooperated with one another in varying combinations to achieve specific community goals, and those of any one region tended to become linked by marriages. Moreover, members of the gentry throughout China seemed to have a community consciousness based on similar backgrounds, similar status, and similar interests. But the gentry had no formal organizations comparable, for example, to the guilds of the commercial and industrial classes. It always remained an unorganized class of independent large families.

The nearest approach to formal inter-family organization among the gentry was association of literati in literary academies (*shu-yuan*) and scholarly societies (*she*), which were common in Ming times and occasionally, especially in the late years of the dynasty, were tinged with political purpose. Such associations were principally intended to provide literary and philosophical edification for the membership, however, and governmental officials regularly fostered their development by making financial contributions and by participating in their activities. When they became centers of political agitation, then academies and societies were vulnerable to charges of treasonable partisanship, and the government suppressed them. Several times during the Ming dynasty, all organizations of these types were outlawed.

Despite not having any large-scale formal organization, the gentry was a powerful force in Ming life. On the whole, it was a conservative force. It was interested in maintaining the agrarian values with which its economic status was associated and upon which peasant acquiescence in its demands was based. It was interested in maintaining social stability and public order, essential both to its prestige and its property rights. It therefore willingly cooperated with the government, for its class interests tended to coincide with the political interests of the government. The Ming government, in its turn, refrained from introducing policies that might upset the local dominance of the gentry. Whereas in previous dynasties there had been repeated attempts to undermine the gentry by land redistribution, limitations on landownership, and the like, and whereas the Ming government did actively curb mercantile and industrial prosperity by instituting its own monopolies and by other repressive policies, there seems to have been no governmental inclination in Ming times to interfere with the status quo in the villages. Only the worst extremes of gentry exploitation were dealt with by the government, to alleviate dangerous peasant discontent or to safeguard its own revenues.

The Amateur Ideal in Ming and Early Ch'ing

The master said, "The accomplished scholar is not a utensil."

—*Lun-yü* II, xii

Another common and important feature of these functions is their *political* character; they do not demand particular, special knowledge, but a *savoir-vivre* and a *savoir-faire*. . . .

—Etienne Balázs, "Les aspects significatifs de la société chinoise," *Asiatische Studien* 6 (1952), 83

While the alien Mongols ruled in China (Yuan dynasty, 1279-1368), Confucian literati were at one of their relatively low points of social importance. The Ming dynasty raised them high again, and as a ruling intelligentsia they naturally cherished an ideal of social stability. As a corollary, in matters of taste they deprecated the idea of change and the quest for originality. By and large, the literati were classicists, like Jonathan Swift in England, and in Swift's defense of the ancients against the moderns, in his vast preference for the humanities over the natural sciences, and in his patrician uneasiness with material utility as the touchstone of value, we see the pattern of literati culture with significant clarity.

Swift died in savage indignation and derangement. The moderns were taking his world and he knew it. Science, progress, business, and utility, the combination he deplored, would soon be leading themes in modern Western culture. But in Ming and early Ch'ing China, the China of the four or five centuries before Westerners came in force, science was slighted, progress denied, business disparaged and (with possibly increasing difficulty) confined; and with these three went the fourth of Swift's desiderata, an anti-vocational retrospective humanism in learning. Artistic style and a cultivated knowledge of the approved canon of ancient works, the "sweetness and light" of a classical love of letters—these, not specialized, "useful" technical training, were the tools of intellectual expression and the keys to social power. These were the qualities mainly tested in the state examinations, which qualified the winners for prestige and opportunities.

From Joseph R. Levenson, *Confucian China and its Modern Fate: The Problem of Intellectual Continuity* (Berkeley and Los Angeles: University of California Press, 1958), pp. 15-19, 41-3. Reprinted by permission of the author, University of California Press, and Routledge and Kegan Paul Ltd., London. Footnotes omitted.

The elite, in short, were not permitted (as Balázs puts it) to "impoverish their personalities in specialization." The Ming style was the amateur style; Ming culture was the apotheosis of the amateur.

Probably more in the Ming period than ever before, as the extreme aestheticism of the Ming eight-legged essay* suggests, Chinese officials were amateurs in office. They were trained academically and (for the most part) tested by written examinations, but they were not trained directly for tasks to be undertaken; whatever the case among aides in official yamens, mere hirelings without the proper Confucianist's claim to leadership, the higher degree-holding members of the bureaucracy—the ruling class par excellence—were not identified with expertise. The prestige of office depended on that fact. The scholar's bellelettristic cultivation, a type of learning divorced from the official tasks for which it qualified him, was essential—not to performance of official functions with technical efficiency (there it was rather inhibiting), but to the cultural celebration of those functions.

If the knowledge characteristic of officials had been a vocational, technical, "useful" knowledge, then it would have been only a professional means, with no intrinsic quality to dignify the bureaucratic end. But when office could be taken to symbolize high culture, knowledge for its own sake, the terminal values of civilization, then office-holding was clearly superior to any other social role. No other sort of success (commercial, military, technological, or the like), which might be assumed to depend on a body of professional knowledge devised as a logical means to produce it, could compete in prestige with success in winning office; for the peculiar preparation for the latter success, by its aesthetic independence, its very irrelevance, logically, to the bureaucratic end—at least in a specialized, technical sense, if not in a broadly moral one—made of that end the end of life. A course in classical letters might train the official ideally to rule by virtuous example—to be himself, as it were, the finest product of art and thought, radiating harmony to society—but it was far from a training in special techniques for effecting social harmony, not by magical sympathy, but by logical consequence.

In China, of course, because of the nature of its institutions,

*The main feature of the civil service examination. It was formalistic in the extreme, with emphasis on literary ingenuity and allusiveness, classical erudition, and a labored process of development by *non sequiturs*. Intellectual originality and practical applicability were discouraged—ED.

this aesthetic brand of knowledge really was for the sake of something: office. But it was a symbolic, not a logical qualification. To see the genuine significance of this distinction, let us compare the Ming situation with the modern English one, for in England, too, classical training has frequently given entrée to civil office. A recent tribute to a British civil servant, after praising his classical scholarship, attempted, rather defensively, it seems, to make an ordinary logical reference of his classical training to his official role:

> He read classics at Malvern and became a humanist. . . . Then in 1932, like many a classical scholar before him, he entered the Home Civil Service. . . . He is certainly a great civil servant, and I have no doubt whatever that he owes his quality to his humanism. It is that which gentles his will and disciplines his mind to the delicacies of human relationships.

Living, as he does, in a highly specialized society, in which the amateur yields to the expert almost all along the line, a society in which "amateur" as a term, in fact, has developed rather its connotation of imperfect skill than of disinterested love, the writer here must strike us as quasi-apologetic (which no Ming classicist, in a similar case, would ever have been) in making such a "professional" plea for the classical curriculum: he writes as though he feels that his public—a practical, vocationally-minded public with a common-sense indifference to educational frills—must be doubting the genuine relevance of antique studies to modern professional tasks. He cannot simply assume a general public acceptance of an obvious affinity between classical education and a managerial office. The prestige of letters, it is true, has lent a greater prestige to the higher bureaucracy in England than it has to its Western counterparts. But in England—and here it has differed from China—the bureaucracy, though thus enhanced, has not been able to reflect its glory back to the source. For while the social facts of Chinese history made bureaucracy the central point of power, the social facts of English history have relegated bureaucracy to a role of service to other powers in the English state. Socially, the rise of "business" (which Swift had seen with such distress), with its anti-traditional, anti-humanist bias, put bureaucracy in the shade, while intellectually it forced the classics from their solitary eminence. To be sure, the nineteenth-century Oxford and Cambridge ideal, like the Confucian, was the educated gentleman, prepared for the world of affairs and his place in the governing class by a course in humane letters, with nothing crudely purposive about it; but this ideal in the Victorian age has been called "almost the sole barrier against an all-encroaching materialism and professionalism." In England, instead of the splendid, symbolic Ming alignment of the highest cultural values with the highest social power, we finally find bureaucracy rather more just a useful employment, while the classics, in so far as they preserve vestigial links with power, tend to be justified as a logically useful means to an end which is only a means itself.

Culture, "the best that has been thought and known" (as Matthew Arnold paraphrased "sweetness and light"), has a bad time in a world of utilitarians. When the "yahoos" and "philistines" of Swift and Arnold dominate society, the defense of culture may tend to lean on philistine criteria. An amateur's love of the liberal arts, his belief that they justify themselves, may be complicated by society's insistence that he find a professional point in their cultivation. But in China, the men of social consequence in the Ming and early Ch'ing periods were hardly cultural philistines; the professional point in their humanistic studies was in their failing to have any specialized professional point. They were amateurs in the fullest sense of the word, genteel initiates in a humane culture, without interest in progress, leanings to science, sympathy for commerce, nor prejudice in favor of utility. Amateurs in government because their training was in art, they had an amateur bias in art itself, for their profession was government.

Long before, in the Sung dynasty, Wang An-shih (1021-86) had tried, among other things, to make the civil-service examinations more practical than aesthetic. Although Wang was unquestionably a dedicated Confucianist, trying to revive in Confucianism its primal concern with political science, his finest official and scholarly contemporaries, who began by largely sharing his convictions, finally turned away, and ordinary Confucianists never forgave him. Was it only impracticability they saw in his sweeping program, or disputable points in his classical exegesis, or an immediate material challenge to their perquisites; or did they also sense that a Confucian landed bureaucracy would rule as intellectual amateurs, or not at all? Had Wang struck a false note, a possible knell for the omnicompetent, socially superior sophisticates, who were no mere scribes in a feudal state, nor professional civil servants in a business one?

Su Tung-p'o (1036-1101), one of the foremost serious opponents of Wang An-shih, seems to have been the first painter to speak of *shih-ta-fu hua,* the "officials' style" in painting, a term which became in the Ming era one of the several interchangeable terms for the "amateur style."

●   ●   ●

The world of painting in early-modern, pre-Western China issued from and reflected a broader world of social institutions. Behind the amateur painter and the southern critic was the anti-professional official, whose socially high estate was the mark of his deeply respected humanistic culture, not a technically specialized one. It was felt, of course, that Confucian moral learning was especially appropriate to government-service, since administration was supposed to be less by law than by example. Still, the official's education failed to make him professional, it was not vocational, for this important reason: his learning was not just valuable for office, but happened to be *the* body of learning, artistic as well as moral, which was valuable in itself, and which lent itself more easily, for examination purposes, to aesthetic exposition than to practical implementation. It was this intimate association of bureaucracy with the mastery of high culture which was cracked by modern Western pressure and its concomitant Chinese nationalism.

When the Chinese nation began to supersede Chinese culture as the focal point of loyalty, sentiments grew for changing, and finally for abandoning, the examination system (this was done in 1905). An education sacrosanct in the old heyday of the amateurs, when "the accomplished scholar was not a utensil," came to be criticized more and more, towards the end of the nineteenth century, as being far too predominantly literary—as failing, that is, to equip officials with specialized, useful knowledge for the national defense. The Chinese state was changing its identity, from that of a world, an environment in which the officials' culture flourished, to that of a nation, whose needs should color its bureaucracy's educational purposes. It meant the end of the "aesthetic value" and self-sufficiency of the bureaucratic Confucian "princely man," which had been at opposite poles (as Weber saw it) from the Puritan—and capitalist—"vocation."

With the pressure, then, of modern Western industrialism (and those attendant concepts—science, progress, business, and utility—unhonored, we have noticed, in the Ming literati culture) on Chinese society and Chinese consciousness, the charge of formalism came to be leveled at the official examinations and at the intellectual ideals which the latter sustained. But objectively, at the time such censure began to be effective, the examinations were not essentially more formalistic than in Ming and early Ch'ing times, when the "eight-legged essay," such a scandal to the moderns, was perfected and prescribed.

Only then (almost only now) was the scholar-official's emphasis on form, on the subtleties of style, in the literati-painting as in the literary essay, generally felt to be the symptom of a weak concern with content. Earlier, the idea had occurred to a few individuals: in the seventeenth century Ku Yen-wu had called the eight-legged essay more harmful than the ancient burning of the books, since it led, in effect, by the prominence given to formal technique, to the destruction of books through their not being read. To rationalistic, insufficiently historically-minded moderns, to whom such criticism appeared incontrovertible, the fact that Ku's views had not prevailed seemed a bad accident or a Manchu Machiavellian achievement. But a less desperate or question-begging explanation than these lies in one's awareness of the amateur ideal as a long-continued condition of Chinese thought. Only when the modern West impinged on China and undermined the position of the gentry-literati-officials, who had set the styles in art and expression as they set the rates in taxes and rents—only then did the concept of "amateur" slide into its modern sense of something less than "specialist," and what had once been precious to traditionalists and classicists seem mainly preciosity to a new youth in a new world of science and revolution.

The Tributary System in Ch'ing

Men from foreign cultures, even more alien to Confucian classical standards than the native "great unwashed," could hardly aspire to the Charmed Circle of the only truly cultured. A tribute system and a tribute-system mentality summed up the Confucian wisdom of "diplomatic relations." Foreign affairs were considered barbarian affairs, and the tribute-system mentality, intellectually aggressive (to say the least), was politically defensive: only preserve the realm that preserved the Charmed Circle. As Teng and Fairbank explain the tribute system, trade and profit, though officially scorned, persistently peeped out from under the cloak of Confucian morality.

From J. K. Fairbank and S. Y. Teng, *Ch'ing Administration: Three Studies* (Cambridge, Mass: Harvard University Press, 1960). © 1960 by the Harvard-Yenching Institute. Reprinted by permission of the publisher. Footnotes omitted.

But Confucian officials, even when they gained surreptitious profit themselves, kept their hands on the cloak and blanketed any revolutionary potential—including (as they contracted their vision to the Middle Kingdom of we-happy-few) the potential for expansion.

For purpose of analysis it may be pointed out (1) that the tributary system was a natural outgrowth of the cultural pre-eminence of the early Chinese, (2) that it came to be used by the rulers of China for political ends of self-defense, (3) that in practice it had a very fundamental and important commercial basis, and (4) that it served as the medium for Chinese international relations and diplomacy. It was, in short, a scheme of things entire, and deserves attention as one historical solution to problems of world organization.

Behind the tributary system as it became institutionalized in the Ming and Ch'ing periods lay the age-old tradition of Chinese cultural superiority over the barbarians. Continuously from the bronze age, when Shang civilization first appears as a culture-island in northern China, this has been a striking element in Chinese thought, perpetuated by the eternal conflict between the settled agrarian society of the Yellow River basin and the pastoral nomads of the steppe beyond the Wall, as well as by the persistent expansion of the Chinese to the south among the tribes whose remnants are now being absorbed in Yunnan and Kweichow. From this contact with the nomads of the north and west and with the aborigines of the south, the Chinese appear to have derived certain basic assumptions which may be stated as follows: first, that Chinese superiority over the barbarians had a cultural rather than a mere political basis; it rested less upon force than upon the Chinese way of life embodied in such things as the Confucian code of conduct and the use of the Chinese written language; the sign of the barbarian was not race or origin so much as non-adherence to this way of life. From this it followed, secondly, that those barbarians who wished to "come and be transformed" (*lai-hua*), and so participate in the benefits of (Chinese) civilization, must recognize the supreme position of the Emperor; for the Son of Heaven represented all mankind, both Chinese and barbarian, in his ritual sacrifices before the forces of nature. Adherence to the Chinese way of life automatically entailed the recognition of the Emperor's mandate to rule all men. This supremacy of the Emperor as mediator between Heaven and Earth was most obviously acknowledged in the performance of the *kotow,* the three kneelings and nine prostrations to which European envoys later objected. It was also acknowledged by the bringing of a tribute of local produce, by the formal bestowal of a seal, comparable to the investiture of a vassal in medieval Europe, and in other ways. Thus the tributary system, as the sum total of these formalities, was the mechanism by which barbarous non-Chinese regions were given their place in the all-embracing Chinese political, and therefore ethical, scheme of things.

This general theory is of course familiar to the most casual student of Chinese history, and yet the realities of the situation are still a matter of dispute. In the intercourse between the Chinese state and the barbarians, commercial relations became inseparably bound up with tributary. Trade was conducted by barbarian merchants who accompanied the tributary envoy to the frontier or even to the capital; sometimes it was conducted by the members of the mission itself. That tribute was a cloak for trade has been a commonplace ever since merchants from the Roman orient arrived in China in A.D. 166 claiming to be envoys of Marcus Aurelius. Thus Benedict de Goez, crossing Central Asia in the year 1604, describes the "sham embassies" of merchants from the Western kingdoms who "forge public letters in the names of the kings whom they profess to represent" and "under pretense of being ambassadors go and offer tribute to the Emperor." Innumerable other examples could be cited wherein tribute, in the minds of the tribute bearers, was merely a formality connected with trade; at Macao and Canton, indeed, the Europeans in their concentration upon the substance of commerce eventually forgot all about the formality which theoretically still went with it.

This economic interpretation, however, is made from the point of view of the barbarians. The motivation of the Court is a different matter.

The argument that the tributary system was developed by the Court chiefly for political defense has been succinctly stated by Dr. T. F. Tsiang:

> Out of this period of intense struggle and bitter humiliation [the eleventh and twelfth centuries], the neo-Confucian philosophy, which began then to dominate China, worked out a dogma in regard to international relations, to hold sway in China right to the middle of the nineteenth century. . . . That dogma asserts that national security could only be found in isolation and stipulates that whoever wished to enter into relations with China must do so as China's vassal, acknowledging the supremacy of the Chinese emperor and obeying his

commands, thus ruling out all possibility of international intercourse on terms of equality. It must not be construed to be a dogma of conquest or universal dominion, for it imposed nothing on foreign peoples who chose to remain outside the Chinese world. It sought peace and security, with both of which international relations were held incompatible. If relations there had to be, they must be of the suzerain-vassal type, acceptance of which meant to the Chinese acceptance of the Chinese ethic on the part of the barbarian. . . .

It must not be assumed that the Chinese Court made a profit out of . . . tribute. The imperial gifts bestowed in return were usually more valuable than the tribute. . . . Chinese statesmen before the latter part of the nineteenth century would have ridiculed the notion that national finance and wealth should be or could be promoted by means of international trade. On China's part the permission to trade was intended to be a mark of imperial bounty and a means of keeping the barbarians in the proper state of submissiveness. . . .

Thus we might conclude that trade and tribute were cognate aspects of a single system of foreign relations, the moral value of tribute being the more important in the minds of the rulers of China, and the material value of trade in the minds of the barbarians; this balance of interests would allow mutual satisfaction and the system would continue to function. From this it might be concluded further that the tributary system really worked in reverse, the submission of the barbarians being actually bought and paid for by the trade conceded to them by China. But this last is an over-simplification which runs counter to the whole set of ideas behind the system, and it also overlooks the interesting possibility, which deserves exploration, of an imperial economic interest—for instance, in the silk export trade. In short it seems impossible at present to make more than one generalization: that the tributary system was a framework within which all sorts of interests, personal and imperial, economic and social, found their expression. Further study should reveal an interplay between greed and statecraft, dynastic policy and vested interest, similar to that in other great political institutions.

19 / JAPAN'S SELF-IMPOSED ISOLATION

Confucian Chinese society was sui generis; *no other Asian society was quite like it. But if Chinese international trade and relations were drawn under the roof of the tribute system, with its politically defensive character, a similar political requirement drew the Japanese back to Japan, in just the age when they might have met the*

Europeans half-way, or a little more than half. Foreign adventures, foreign relations seemed to threaten the hard-won Japanese order, under the new Tokugawa shogunate in the seventeenth century.

In Europe, expansion overseas seems to have been a concomitant of nation-building, nourished by peace and unity after internecine warfare (cf. Spain after the union of crowns and the conquest of Granada, the consolidation of the English state under the Tudors, the Bourbon accession to power in France and the end of the religious wars, the rise of the Dutch Republic when the Spaniards lost their hold). But in Japan, the Tokugawa could never make themselves Japan incarnate. They only won hegemony among a congeries of fiefs, and even then they had to strain to keep it (until 1868). The "Bakufu" (shogunate) was not a government that could establish a sense of national identity and purpose. Foreign contacts and Japanese expansion, which threatened to nurture, not a greater Japan, but fiefs intent on a lesser Tokugawa, were finally discouraged by the Bakufu, as it turned—with Japan—decisively inward. The next pair of selections describes the turning.

The Potential to Expand

It will be seen that the civilization of Japan was formed in comparative seclusion, and this has given it a very special character. Its many foreign elements were borrowed in such circumstances that they could not overcome a stubborn indigenous sentiment, and even until modern times Japanese life has preserved much of its earliest native quality. No nation has been more ready to consider new teaching, and yet none has been more tenacious of its own tradition. These circumstances have given rise to an impression, which a cursory study of history seems to confirm, that the geographical isolation of Japan has fostered a habit of seclusion, an aversion from foreign intercourse. But there is little to justify this opinion. From earliest times relationships with China and Korea, sometimes peaceful, sometimes warlike, were continuous despite an occasional diplomatic rupture, and from the end of the feudal wars in the twelfth century, when internal peace was established, there was a steady increase and extension of Japanese maritime enterprise. Recent researches have established that Japanese ships (from the Luchu islands) visited Java, Sumatra, Siam, and Malacca in the fifteenth and probably in the late fourteenth century. From that time onwards Japanese vessels in legitimate or

From Sir George B. Sansom, *The Western World and Japan* (London: The Cresset Press Ltd., 1950), pp. 179-80. Reprinted by permission of the publisher.

piratical trade sailed freely in Far Eastern waters and Japanese merchants or soldiers of fortune were to be found in most Far Eastern cities. It was during the early phases of a movement of Japanese expansion that the first Europeans arrived in Japan; and the welcome accorded to Portuguese missionaries and traders, so friendly in contrast to their treatment in China and some other Asiatic countries, is to be explained by the enthusiasm for overseas adventure and trade which then prevailed among the feudal leaders of Japan.

Had the Portuguese and other Europeans not arrived upon the scene in the sixteenth century, it is quite probable that the Japanese within a few decades would have established themselves in Formosa, the Philippines, and parts of Indonesia, thus forming the nucleus of a colonial empire in the Pacific. But such designs, which were certainly harbored by Japanese rulers, had to be abandoned when it was thought that Western guns and ships might be turned against Japan by the foreigners. It was no failure of the expansive impulse, but only a reluctant recognition of weakness that caused Japan to withdraw into almost complete seclusion in 1640. The hazard which brought Western influence into the Pacific before Japan had achieved a stable central government thus gave the maritime countries a free hand in the Far East and so fixed for centuries the pattern of colonial enterprise in that region. During those centuries the rulers of Japan abandoned all dreams of empire, and only by exception did a few unorthodox thinkers turn their minds to a day when Japan might renew her broken intercourse with foreign countries. The energies of the governing class were devoted entirely to the consolidation of their power and to devising instruments by which to preserve it. Theirs was a policy of almost complete isolation.

The Decision to Withdraw

[The Shogun] . . . was enthusiastic in the promotion of foreign trade, and the first decades of the seventeenth century saw a rapid expansion of Japanese activity abroad. The Bakufu issued licenses for the voyages of Japanese merchant vessels under the shogun's vermilion seal, while individual Japanese traders and other adventurers found their way to most countries in the western Pacific

From Sir George B. Sansom, *A History of Japan, 1615-1867* (Stanford: Stanford University Press, 1963; London: The Cresset Press Ltd., 1964), pp. 35-6, 42-4. © 1963 by the Board of Trustees of the Leland Stanford Junior University. Reprinted by permission of the publishers. Footnotes omitted.

and beyond the Malacca Straits to Burma. The number of licenses issued between 1604 and 1635 was of the order of three hundred, or an average of ten voyages out and home each year. This was a fairly large number in a period of very slow transport by sea. In addition to these licensed carriers, Portuguese and Chinese ships carried both imports and exports, while the western daimyos, especially Shimazu, Matsuura, Nabeshima, and Omura, traded in licensed vessels on their own account from time to time.

The behavior of some of the licensed ships was almost piratical. They would attack any ship or place for booty, and they were feared in all parts of Southeast Asia. Several countries protested and pressed the Japanese government to take measures of control. At the request of Luzon the visits of the licensed ships were reduced to four a year. Some writers regard this action as a prelude to the exclusion policy developed in the 1640s.

The export cargoes consisted mainly of silver, copper, iron, sulphur, camphor, rice, and other grains, as well as substantial quantities of lacquer goods, fans, and similar works of handicraft. In return traders brought to Japan raw silk (the most important item), silk fabrics of high quality, cotton, sharkskin, deerskin, scented woods, dyes, sugar, lead, and tin.

There were Japanese settlements in most parts of eastern Asia, from Formosa and Macao to the Moluccas, the Philippines, Borneo, Celebes and Java, Siam and the Malay Peninsula. The largest were in Luzon, Siam, and Indochina. Many of the settlers were soldiers who could find no suitable employment at home after the wars. Among them was one Yamada Nagamasa (d. 1633), who lived in the Siamese capital of Ayuthia, where he was trusted as an adviser by the King and appointed to high office. He was able by his military skill to suppress an outbreak of revolt during a succession dispute. . . .

This thriving and promising phase of expansion came to a surprising end upon the issue of certain orders closing the country to foreign trade and travel with a few strictly limited exceptions. These orders, of 1633, 1635, and 1639, are often loosely described as the three Exclusion Decrees. This is not quite accurate, since in form they were not public notices but letters of instruction to provincial officers directing them how to carry out the policy of the central government.

. . . The contents of these documents . . . show the gradual development of a policy of almost complete isolation—an historical phenomenon which, while simple in appearance, is by no means easily explained. They are akin to the anti-Christian orders issued by Ieyasu in the years 1611-14, but they are much more drastic and much wider in scope.

. . .

. . . [The] documents of 1633-39 clearly state that the purpose of the exclusion edicts was the suppression of Christianity in Japan. Since the teachings of the missionaries were incompatible with the feudal principles upon which the power of the Bakufu was based, the persecution of the priests and their converts, though morally evil, might be defended on political grounds; but it could scarcely be argued that it was necessary to close the country altogether in order to keep out the influence of a foreign religion.

Evidently there are some anomalies here. In the first place, the exclusion policy was not thoroughgoing, since it made exceptions for China and Holland, in fact for any country that did not send Christian missionaries to Japan. The Dutch, anxious to capture the Japan trade, had been at pains to warn the Japanese against the Portuguese and the Spanish, whom they accused of planning to seize Japanese territory or at least to use force against Japan. The English traders would not have been excluded, but they had already left Hirado (the center of their activities) in 1623, before the exclusion orders. Thus the effect desired by the Bakufu could have been secured by the existing ban upon the entry of Portuguese or Spanish persons, whether traders or missionaries.

The Spanish had been denied entry after 1624. And, as mentioned, all foreign residents were ordered in 1636 to move to Deshima at the head of Nagasaki Bay, where lodging was prepared for them. This applied only to a few Portuguese, who were expelled from the country in 1638, following the Shimabara rising. Moreover, by the time of the third and final exclusion order of 1639, Christianity had been all but entirely stamped out, and it would have been possible to prevent the entry of missionaries by a systematic control at the ports. This, however, would have required the collaboration of the daimyos in whose territory the ports were situated; and here we have a further clue to the policy of the Bakufu.

The Tozama daimyos in western Japan and Kyushu profited by foreign trade, and if they were allowed to continue their trading they might easily grow strong enough to endanger the primacy of the Bakufu and even bold enough to call upon Portuguese or

Spanish assistance. The only way of preventing such rivalry was to prohibit all foreign trade at ports other than Nagasaki, which was under the direct jurisdiction of the Bakufu. In this way the Bakufu obtained not only a control of foreign trade but also a monopoly of its profits; and whatever other result was expected from the exclusion policy, it is quite clear that this is exactly what the shogun had been aiming at since Ieyasu's day. In retrospect it becomes evident that Tokugawa policy was directed to creating a dictatorship, an authoritarian state, exercising full control over all aspects of the national life, economic as well as social and moral.

Was the Bakufu's fear of Christian propaganda genuine, or was it a pretense by which the exclusion policy was justified? The number of Japanese Christians, probably of the order of 300,000 before the great persecutions, may have fallen by death and apostasy to far less than 100,000 men and women who practiced their devotions in concealment. It is hard to believe that a man of the stature of Ieyasu would have been deterred from his policy of expansion by fear of the influence of so small and weak a community as the scattered Christians after 1625. But neither Hidetada nor Iemitsu was cast in the heroic mold, and it is probable that they and their advisers genuinely feared foreign aggression. They were not men to take a great risk. They had no trust in the loyalty of the Outside Lords, and what they had heard of the activities of European states did not encourage them to join in the struggle for territories and trade which was disturbing the Pacific Ocean.

There is an illuminating passage in a report of François Caron, the head of the Dutch trading station in Japan, who had given some lessons in world geography to Iemitsu. Writing in 1641, Caron says that "after investigating the size of the world, the multitude of its countries and the smallness of Japan . . . he [Iemitsu] was greatly surprised and heartily wished that his land had never been visited by any Christian."

. . .

But it is unlikely that fear of Christianity was the compelling reason for the seclusion policy. There is interesting evidence on this point in an account by a Ming scholar, Huang Tsung-hsi, of his visit to Japan in about 1646, when he sought to obtain help for resistance against the Manchus. He discusses the Japanese seclusion policy and agrees that fear of Christianity and of Europeans was a motive, but says that the underlying reason was the determination of the Tokugawa to secure internal peace and prosperity, and to avoid any foreign involvement likely to jeopardize those aims.

The lengths to which the Bakufu went in enforcing this policy seem to confirm Huang's view. The measures they took were typical of Confucian China, which was always isolationist and preoccupied with internal security, and especially typical of Ming China, which dismantled its navy, closed its ports, and restricted trade to stations where it could be closely regulated.

20 / THE OTTOMANS FALL BACK

What had happened to Muslim prospects of besting the Europeans? Whereas in China and (in a different way) in Japan social and political structure and circumstances damaged the will to expand, in the Ottoman Empire, as the next selection suggests, they damaged the ability. The ability of the Far Eastern countries, too, might have been impaired if they had been as close as the Ottomans to massive hostile military forces. But as it was, in the face of the merest vanguard of European power, the Chinese and Japanese retrenchment seems an act of self-denial more than a yielding to interdiction.

In the sixteenth century the Ottoman Empire reached the limits of its expansion, and came up against barriers which it could not pass. On the eastern border, despite the victories in the field of Selim I and Suleyman, the Ottoman armies could not advance into Persia. The new centralized monarchy of the Safavids, then at the peak of their power; the high plateau of Iran, posing new problems of logistics and calling for new and unfamiliar techniques; the difficulties of leading against a Muslim adversary an army whose traditions since its birth were of the holy war against the infidels—all these combined to halt the Ottoman forces at the frontiers of Iran, and cut them off from overland expansion into central Asia or India.

In Eastern waters they encountered the stout ships of the Portuguese, whose shipbuilders and navigators, trained to meet the challenge of the Atlantic, were more than a match for the calm-

From Bernard Lewis, *The Emergence of Modern Turkey* (London and New York: Oxford University Press [under the auspices of the Royal Institute of International Affairs], 1961), pp. 24-5, 27-8, 31-2, 34-6. Reprinted by permission of the publisher. Footnotes omitted.

water ships of the Ottomans. Stouter vessels, more guns, better seamanship were what defeated the successive attempts of the Ottomans to break out of the ring, and swept Muslim shipping from the waters of the Indian Ocean.

In the Crimea and the lands beyond it they were halted by Russia. In 1475 the Ottomans had conquered Kaffa. Part of the Crimean coast passed under direct Ottoman rule, the Giray Khans of the Tatars became Ottoman vassals, and in 1569 the Ottomans even launched a plan to open a canal between the Don and Volga and thus, by acquiring a shipping route to central Asia, to break out of the Portuguese noose. But here too the Ottomans found their way blocked. At the same time as western Europe was expanding by sea around Africa and into Asia, eastern Europe was expanding by land across the steppe, southward and eastward towards the lands of Islam. In 1502 the once mighty khanate of the Golden Horde was finally extinguished, and much of its territory absorbed by Russia. The successor khanates of Kazan, Astrakhan, and Crimea lingered on for a while, but before long the Russians were able to conquer the first two, and to exercise a growing pressure on the third. The way was open to the Black Sea and the North Caucasus, the Caspian and western Siberia, where the advance of Russia barred and enclosed the Ottomans as did the Portuguese and their successors in the eastern seas.

In Africa, desert, mountain, and climate offered obstacles which there was no incentive to surmount, while in the Mediterranean, after a brief interval, naval supremacy was lost to the maritime countries of the West.

But the classical area of Ottoman expansion had been in none of these. Since the first crossing of the Bosporus in the mid-fourteenth century, Europe had been the promised land of the Ottomans—the "House of War" par excellence, in which the power and the glory of Islam were to be advanced by victorious battle against the infidel. On 27 September 1529, after conquering Hungary, the armies of Suleyman the Magnificent reached Vienna—and on 15 October they began to withdraw from the still unconquered city. The event was decisive. For another century-and-a-half inconclusive warfare was waged for Hungary, and in 1683 yet another attempt, the last, was made against Vienna. But the cause was already lost. The Ottoman Empire had reached the line beyond which it could not advance, from which it could only withdraw. The valor of the Habsburg, as of the Safavid armies, no doubt played its part in stemming the Ottoman onslaught, but **is** insufficient as an explanation of why the defenders of Vienna were able to halt the victors of Kossovo, Varna, Nicopolis, and Mohacs. There too we may perhaps find an explanation in the problems of a new and different terrain, calling for new techniques of warfare and especially of supply and transport.

• • •

While the great Ottoman war-machine, extended beyond its range, was grinding to a standstill in the plains of Hungary, the life and growth of the Ottoman Empire were being circumvented, on a far vaster scale, by the oceanic voyages of discovery of the Western maritime peoples, the ultimate effect of which was to turn the whole eastern Mediterranean area, where the Empire was situated, into a backwater. In 1555 the Imperial ambassador in Constantinople, Ogier Ghiselin de Busbecq, one of the acutest European observers of Turkey, could still comment that the western Europeans basely squandered their energies "seeking the Indies and the Antipodes across vast fields of ocean, in search of gold," and abandoning the heart of Europe to imminent and almost certain conquest. But in about 1580 an Ottoman geographer, in an account of the New World written for Murad III, gave warning of the dangers to the Islamic lands and the disturbance to Islamic trade resulting from the establishment of Europeans on the coasts of America, India, and the Persian Gulf; he advised the sultan to open a canal through the isthmus of Suez and send a fleet "to capture the ports of Hind and Sind and drive away the infidels." By 1625 another Ottoman observer, a certain Omer Talib, could see the danger in a more pressing form:

> Now the Europeans have learnt to know the whole world; they send their ships everywhere and seize important ports. Formerly, the goods of India, Sind, and China used to come to Suez, and were distributed by Muslims to all the world. But now these goods are carried on Portuguese, Dutch, and English ships to Frangistan, and are spread all over the world from there. What they do not need themselves they bring to Istanbul and other Islamic lands, and sell it for five times the price, thus earning much money. For this reason gold and silver are becoming scarce in the lands of Islam. The Ottoman Empire must seize the shores of Yemen and the trade passing that way; otherwise before very long, the Europeans will rule over the lands of Islam.

The effects on Middle Eastern trade of the circumnavigation of Africa were by no means as immediate and as catastrophic as was at one time believed. Right through the sixteenth century Eastern merchandise continued to reach the Ottoman Empire, coming by ship to Red Sea ports and Basra and overland across Persia, and European merchants came to Turkey to buy. But the volume of international trade passing this way was steadily decreasing. From the seventeenth century, the establishment of Dutch and British power in Asia and the transference of the routes of world trade to the open ocean deprived Turkey of the greater part of her foreign commerce and left her, together with the countries over which she ruled, in a stagnant backwater through which the life-giving stream of world trade no longer flowed.

．　．　．

. . . The fall in money and rise of prices, the growing cost of government and warfare, the sale of offices and farming of taxes —all these are known in other Mediterranean and adjoining states [as well as in Turkey], where they contributed to the rise of a new class of capitalists and financiers, with a growing and constructive influence on governments.

In Turkey too there were rich merchants and bankers, such as the Greek Michael Cantacuzenos and the Portuguese Jew Joseph Nasi—the Fugger of the Orient, as Braudel called him. But they were never able to play anything like the financial, economic, and political role of their European counterparts. Part of the cause of this must undoubtedly be found in the progressive stagnation of Ottoman trade, to which allusion has already been made. But that is not all. Most if not all of these merchants were Christians or Jews—tolerated but second-class subjects of the Muslim state. However great their economic power, they were politically penalized and socially segregated; they could obtain political power only by stealth, and exercise it only by intrigue, with demoralizing effect on all concerned. Despite the scale and extent of their financial operations, they were unable to create political conditions more favorable to commerce, or to build up any solid structure of banking and credit, and thus help the Ottoman government in its perennial financial straits. In England too finance and credit were at first in the hands of alien specialists, who have left their name in Lombard Street. But these were ousted in time by vigorous and pushful native rivals. In Turkey no such rivals arose, and in any case, in the general decline of the seventeenth century, even the Greek and Jewish merchant princes of Constantinople dwindled into insignificance. Fortunes were still made in Turkey, but their origin was not economic. Mostly they were political or fiscal in origin, obtained through the holding of public office. Nor were they spent on investment or development, but consumed or hoarded, after the fashion of the time.

•   •   •

Classical Islamic civilization, like others before and after it, including our own, was profoundly convinced of its superiority and self-sufficiency. In its earliest, primitive phase, Islam had been open to influences from the Hellenistic Orient, from Persia, even from India and China. Many works were translated into Arabic from Greek, Syriac, and Persian. But with the solitary exception of the late Latin chronicle of Orosius, not a single translation into a Muslim language is known of any Latin or Western work until the sixteenth century, when one or two historical and geographical works were translated into Turkish. For the Muslim of classical times, Frankish Europe was an outer darkness of barbarism and unbelief, from which the sunlit world of Islam had nothing to learn and little to fear. This view, though becoming outdated toward the end of the Middle Ages, was transmitted by the medieval Muslims to their Ottoman heirs, and was reinforced by the crushing victories of Ottoman arms over their European opponents. On the warlike but open frontier one could still exchange lessons with one's counterpart on the other side; through renegades and refugees new skills could still reach the Islamic Empire. But the willingness to learn these lessons was not there, and in time the sources also dried up. Masked by the still imposing military might of the Ottoman Empire, the peoples of Islam continued to cherish the dangerous but comfortable illusion of the immeasurable and immutable superiority of their own civilization to all others—an illusion from which they were slowly shaken by a series of humiliating military defeats.

In the military empire, at once feudal and bureaucratic, which they had created, the Muslims knew only four professions—government, war, religion, and agriculture. Industry and trade were left to the non-Muslim conquered subjects, who continued to practice their inherited crafts. Thus the stigma of the infidel became attached to the professions which the infidels followed, and remained so attached even after many of the craftsmen had become Muslim. Westerners and native Christians, bankers, merchants, and craftsmen, were all involved in the general contempt which made the Ottoman Muslim impervious to ideas or inventions of

Christian origin and unwilling to bend his own thoughts to the problems of artisans and vile mechanics. Primitive techniques of production, primitive means of transportation, chronic insecurity and social penalization, combined to preclude any long-term or large-scale undertakings, and to keep the Ottoman economy at the lowest level of competence, initiative, and morality.

.   .   .

In the late Middle Ages, the Ottoman Empire was the only state in Europe which already possessed the territory, the cohesion, the organization, the manpower, and the resources to carry the new apparatus of warfare, the crushing cost of which was outmoding the city states and feudal principalities of medieval Europe, as surely as modern weapons have outmoded the petty sovereignties of Europe in our own day. In part perhaps because of that very primacy, it failed to respond to the challenge which produced the nation-states of sixteenth-century Europe, and the great commercial and technological efflorescence of which they were the scene.

Fundamentally, the Ottoman Empire had remained or reverted to a medieval state, with a medieval mentality and a medieval economy—but with the added burden of a bureaucracy and a standing army which no medieval state had ever had to bear. In a world of rapidly modernizing states it had little chance of survival.

21 / MUSLIM AND HINDU FAILURES IN THE EAST INDIES

And so, although Muslims were prominent in Asia east of the Ottoman Empire, well-entrenched and reasonably well-equipped with economic and other techniques, the greatest Muslim political power was out of the contest in those Eastern target-areas of European enterprise. Even so, when no significant countervailing Muslim state power was available, when the Portuguese were the marksmen the targets were hard to knock over. As the first extract emphasizes, Muslim and Hindu commercial practices were sophisticated enough to accommodate newcomers. But in the last analysis, as the second extract demonstrates, the Muslim social context of commerce was not a supporting one; there was no real basis for an adequate defense against European incursions in Asia, much less a basis for Muslim incursions into Europe.

The Indigenous Commercial Structure: Strength

. . . After journeying through the inhospitable seas of southern Africa the Portuguese ships had come into regions [i.e., the Muslim lands of Southeast Asia], where there was a complex of shipping, trade, and authority as highly developed as the European: forms of political capitalism at least as large in dimensions as those of southern Europe, and probably larger; shipping in bottoms many of them carrying more than those used in European merchant shipping; a trade in every conceivable valuable high-quality product carried on by a great multitude of traders; merchant gentlemen and harbor princes wielding as great financial power as did the merchants and princes of Europe. By conquering the chief strategic points on the Asian sea routes, the Portuguese succeeded in establishing a colonial domain in that world, a weak empire which nevertheless was able to maintain itself with great vitality for a century. The Portuguese colonial regime, built by and upon war, coercion, and violence, did not at any point signify a stage of "higher development" economically for Asian trade. The traditional commercial structure continued to exist, however much damaged by religious wars breaking out between Muslims and Christians. Trade did not undergo any increase in quantity worthy of mention in the period. The commercial and economic forms of the Portuguese colonial regime were the same as those of Asian trade and Asian authority: a trade relatively small in volume, conducted by the government as a private enterprise, and all further exercise of authority existing only to insure the financial, fiscal exploitation of trade, shipping, and port traffic, with the higher officials and religious dignitaries recruited from the Portuguese aristocracy. Official exploitation, the economic policy of the colonial regime, was feudal, then, not bourgeois-commercial. The farming of revenues on a large scale in practice transferred the exploitation to the Indian and Persian Moslem wealthy merchants. The ordinary Portuguese "free burghers"—to use the Dutch Company term —carried on their handiwork, shipping, and craft trading side-by-side with and together with Asians. Ethnic intermixture took place on a large scale.

The Portuguese colonial regime, then, did not introduce a single

From J. C. van Leur, "On Early Asian Trade," *Indonesian Trade and Society: Essays in Asian Social and Economic History* (The Hague: W. van Hoeve Ltd, 1955), pp. 117-19. Reprinted by permission of the publisher. Footnotes omitted.

new economic element into the commerce of southern Asia. The forms of political and economic domination—monopolies, financial exploitation, "fiscalization" of the government—all of them originated in the caliphates and Byzantium, and were transferred to Portugal, and perhaps carried on there, by Jews and Italians. The political power of the Portuguese, based on their military superiority, now made possible the large-scale application of those forms in Asia. That military superiority was the only thing the Portuguese carried overseas to Asia as a new and European element. Though the Portuguese period was the first of the European colonial periods which from then on were to decide the fate of Asia, this fact serves to separate it from the following, second period, that of Dutch and English overseas voyages and colonial settlement, and to link it in spirit and forms to the previous periods, those of purely Asian trade. The Portuguese regime only introduced a non-intensive drain on the existing structure of shipping and trade. The next period would in its time organize a new system of foreign trade and foreign shipping, it would call into life trenchant colonial relationships, and it would create new economic forms in Europe—not perhaps as a direct result but rather as a parallel development bolstered by the system. Not Lisbon and Seville, but Amsterdam, Middelburg, Enkhuizen, and London were among the heralds of a new era.

The Indigenous Commercial Structure: Weakness

The group of important merchants in Malacca included some very rich and powerful people, in particular Javanese merchants and Hindu merchants from southern India. Barbosa's criterion of a very rich merchant is someone who can buy the cargoes of three or four ships carrying all sorts of valuable goods and then load his ships with goods from his private stocks of merchandise. The *bendahara* Ninan Chata (Chetti?), also mentioned by Barros in his *Da Asia*, who originally stood high in Portuguese favor, was one of these powerful merchants. Pires describes the trade carried on with the Moluccas by the Hindu, Curia Deva. Most writers of those days are unanimous in acclaiming the business talent displayed by the Hindus. Pires praises it highly when discussing Hindu trade in Cambay and he probably thought equally well of the Hindus in

From M. A. P. Meilink-Roelofsz, *Asian Trade and European Influence in the Indonesian Archipelago between 1500 and about 1630* (The Hague: Martinus Nijhoff, 1962), pp. 55-7. Reprinted by permission of the publisher. Footnotes omitted.

southern India and also of those established in Malacca. He compares them with the Italians of his day in their knowledge and the way they handled their merchandise. Their business tactics were on a high level and he comments on their efficient system of bookkeeping. None of the Moslem merchants in Cambay could compete with them in commercial ability and Pires advises young Portuguese who wish to become clerks to apprentice themselves to the Hindu merchants of Gujarat "because the business of trade is a science in itself." Thomas Bowrey who became acquainted with Hindu traders in the second half of the seventeenth century expresses himself equally enthusiastically: "Those that are tradesmen are very ingenious and those that are accomplished merchants are very accute and the most excellent arithmeticins [arithmeticians] in the world." In Malabar, overseas trade was entirely in Moslem hands and, according to Pires, the merchants employed "heathen" *nairs* who accompanied them on their voyages. The *nairs* helped the Moslems in their business administration and could calculate even better than the Moslems themselves.

We learn about the appearance and habits of the patrician Hindu merchants in Malacca from Barbosa's *Book*. They were wealthy and well-fed: "There are here also merchants of Choromandel, who are very corpulent with big bellies, they go bare above the waist and wear cotton clothes below." Besides town houses which served as their places of business, they owned country residences, some of them veritable pleasure gardens surrounded by orchards and gardens with ornamental lakes, and "possessing many slaves, with women and children in separate quarters, but all obedient to the orders of the head of the family, these merchants led a very pleasant life there. Cultured and well-educated, they practiced music and the arts of love."

Both Barros and Pires paint a grimmer picture of the important Javanese merchants. Characteristic of the position which they might occupy in Malaccan society is the power exercised by the Javanese, Utimuti raja, who had many slaves and a fortified settlement in Upeh. Barros holds that only the sultan possessed more goods and slaves than this Utimuti raja who, after the city changed hands, became one of the most dangerous opponents of the Portuguese. Compared with him, the Javanese who had authority over his fellow-countrymen in and around Grise was only a minor figure. Utimuti raja exploited his position shamelessly, according to Barros at least. He compelled the merchants who owed him obedience to sell him goods at prices he fixed himself and he forced all the slaves he could lay his hands on to enter his own service. Since he controlled rice supplies to Malacca and the stocks of this article in the city itself, he had a powerful weapon at his command for protecting his own interests.

Pires estimates the number of Moslem Gujarati in Malacca at one thousand, a large figure and one which should be regarded with some scepticism. Some of these people, too, possessed considerable capital but Pires does not give any examples of individual commercial success as he does in the case of the Hindus and Javanese, and we may therefore assume that the Gujarati were mostly small-time traders. This must also have been the case with the Parsees, Bengali, and Arabs, whose number is estimated by Pires at not less than three thousand. Could a distinction perhaps be made in Malacca, too, between those who were mainly engaged in trade outside Indonesia and those who limited their activities to trade within the confines of the archipelago?

Many an emigrant from Bengal must have settled in Malacca, for Pires notes that a great many Bengali lived there, both men and women. They were simple folk, most of whom earned their living not as merchants but as fishermen or tailors, although their workmanship did not have a very good name.

In spite of all the display of power and wealth and although they had their own jurisdiction, when all was said and done the foreign mercantile community in Malacca was still completely at the mercy of the ruler, who could lay claim to their daughters for his harem and to their estates after death. How utterly different from the position at that time in western Europe where the important merchants were citizens with autonomous rights and civil freedoms.

22 / THE COMMERCIAL INCENTIVES FOR EUROPE AND ASIA

Not only was the home environment less favorable for Asian merchants than for European. Comparatively, there was an Asian deficiency in motive—not in religious motive, nor drive to indulge a zestful spirit, but in the pull of a prize that justified the effort. In the beginning of the age of expansion Asian spices lured Europeans, and the expansion, accordingly, was Europe's. There was no corresponding lure in the West for Asians. The next pair of extracts speaks of the commercial bait in Asia for Europeans, and the disinclination of Asians, in this crucial early stage, to snap at the products of Europe.

Of course, for Europe to act in accordance with its needs, to expand in Asia, Europe must have recognized its deficiencies, discovered where it could remedy the lack, and created a social climate propitious for venture capital. Need alone (any factor alone) is insufficient explanation of the different courses, Western and Eastern, that we see in modern history. But if expansion could not have occurred without an expanded scope for venture capital (as distinct from the creaming of capital in Asia), there had to be something to venture for.

Europe to Asia: European Demand for an Asian Commodity

It is a commonplace of economic history that the farming communities of Europe, down to the late seventeenth century at least, suffered from a chronic shortage of winter feed for cattle. Large numbers of beasts had to be slaughtered every autumn, and the meat preserved for winter consumption by being salted or pickled. Hence the constant and insatiable demand for spices as condiments and preservatives. Salt was the commonest and cheapest preservative (though not particularly cheap by modern standards) and much of the salt supply of western Europe came from Portugal. Apart from salt, the preservative spices were all produced in tropical countries: pepper, the commonest spice, in India, the East Indies, and (a very inferior sort) West Africa; cinnamon in Ceylon, nutmeg and mace in Celebes and other East Indian islands, whence they were shipped from the port of Macassar. Ginger is a Chinese product, though an inferior kind was also grown in Malabar. The most valuable preservative spice—cloves —came from the most restricted producing area, a few small islands in the Molucca group, including Tidore, Ternate, Amboina, and the Banda islands. To complete the list of Eastern trade goods, it is convenient to group together with spices certain other products which commanded high prices in Europe and which went there by the same routes; Chinese silk; Indian cotton cloth; rhubarb,

From J. H. Parry, *The Establishment of the European Hegemony, 1415-1715: Trade and Exploration in the Age of the Renaissance* (New York: Harper & Row, Publishers, Inc. [Harper Torchbooks], 1961), pp. 36-8. Originally published as *Europe and a Wider World* (London: Hutchinson & Company Ltd. [Hutchinson University Library], 1949). Reprinted by permission of the publishers.

grown in China and much prized as a medicine; and precious stones of various kinds—emeralds from India, rubies from Tibet, and sapphires from Ceylon.

The development of the spice trade in the fifteenth century was closely bound up with the expansion of Islam, both westward and eastward, at the expense both of Christian and Hindu. The Ottoman Turks were terrorizing eastern Europe. Other central Asian peoples were pressing into India. A series of foreign Muslim dynasties had long been established at Delhi, and a string of loosely organized Muslim sultanates ruled the west coast as far south as Goa. Only in the south the wealthy and powerful kingdom of Vijayanagar survived as the principal stronghold of Hindu power. At the same time Islam was expanding by sea. Arab colonists had long controlled the towns and trade of East Africa as far south as Mozambique. Muslim traders were spreading their religion through the East Indies and establishing trading principalities. Petty sultans, often Malay in race, usually Muslim in religion, set up as merchant princes in the principal spice-producing islands. Wherever the European Christians went in the East they found that the Muslims had gone before them, and by 1500 both the production of spices and the trade in spices were largely in Muslim hands.

A considerable part of the trade between East and West in the Middle Ages had been carried across Asia overland. As far as western Europe was concerned the activities of the Turks greatly reduced the importance of this route. It is with the seaborne eastern trade that we are primarily concerned. At its eastern end, the trade was handled by the Chinese, whose junks collected the cloves, mace, and nutmeg of the East Indies and carried them to the great Malayan port of Malacca. From Malacca across the Bay of Bengal to India, the trade had fallen by 1500 into the hands of Muslim merchants, whether Indian, Malay, or Arab. In India, the Far Eastern cargoes, together with the cinnamon of Ceylon and the pepper of India itself, were sold in the spice ports of the Malabar coast—Cochin, Calicut, Cananore, Goa—and farther north in the ports of Gujerat, particularly Diu. The population of these ports was mainly Hindu, though some of them, including Diu and Goa, had Muslim overlords. Their trade with the rest of the Indian Ocean littoral was largely handled by the Arabs and by Muslim peoples subject to them. The merchant houses of Arabia, Egypt, and East Africa maintained warehouses and resident factors, paying the local rulers for the privilege. To Malabar they brought horses from Mesopotamia and copper from Arabia. From Malabar their dhows cleared with immensely valuable cargoes for the harbors of the Red Sea and the Persian Gulf, whence the spices having been carried overland to Alexandria or the Syrian ports, and having paid heavy tolls in Cairo or Baghdad, were bought by Venetian merchants for distribution throughout Europe. The costs of the trade were enormous; but so were the profits. It was said that a merchant could ship six cargoes and lose five, but still make a profit when the sixth was sold.

Europe to Asia: Asian Demand for a European Service

The extension of the [English] East India Company's activities to the European continent had its origin in the problem of marketing and selling its imports from Asia. But the development of its port-to-port trade in the Indies, on the other hand, was closely connected with the question of acquiring purchasing power to pay for these imports, the great bulk of which, in the early years, consisted of spices. Both the English and the Dutch realized soon after their arrival in the Indies that European goods were not to be sold in large quantities in Java, Sumatra, or the Moluccas, the chief suppliers of pepper and spices, and that it was not profitable either to drive a trade in these commodities for cash. The indigenous trading system in Southeast Asia and the Indian Ocean was based upon the exchange of Indian textiles for the spices of the East Indies. Participation in the "country trade" by the Europeans was not only a sound commercial policy in view of the high profits which such transactions offered—profits from which part at least of the purchases for Europe could be made—but it also promised to provide some solution to the vexed question of bullion export from Europe engendered by the inability of the latter to sell goods of European production. It was this awareness that the success of the direct trade between England and the Indies depended to a considerable extent upon taking advantage of the existing trading pattern in Asia that led the East India Company to set up a network of trading stations from the Red Sea to Japan. This venture into the "country trade" of Asia posed problems of communication and of organization which in magnitude and complexity surpassed those previously known in English foreign trade.

From K. N. Chaudhuri, *The English East India Company: the Study of an Early Joint-Stock Company 1600-1640* (London: Frank Cass & Co. Ltd., 1965), p. 14. Reprinted by permission of the publisher. Footnotes omitted.

23 / THE LIQUIDATION OF FEUDALISM
AS A PRELUDE TO EXPANSION: PORTUGAL

When Asia did come around to seeking European things, these were capital equipment and its products, the fruits of the very technology that had brought Europe to Asia instead of the reverse. This technology may not have been crucially superior to Asian technology when the expansion process began. But it was a dynamic technology in Europe, its development fostered by the social forces that were also fostering the development of commerce to the point of seeking and finally making a true world market. Societies in Asia, meanwhile, were only battening on their own impressive, perhaps potentially world-wide commerce, not fattening it into actual world-wide shape.

The liberation of commerce from the "fetters of feudalism" began with the fettering of feudalism. Monarchy, striving to enhance its central power at the expense of landed-aristocratic privilege, was a natural ally of cities and "bourgeoisie." (In the seventeenth-century Netherlands, where the Dutch Republic won its independence from the Spanish Hapsburg monarchy, the revolt neverthe-less had an anti-feudal ambiance of "urban and class liberties," and one of its manifestations was aggressive commercial expansion, which extended to expansion overseas.) The provocative existence of feudalism was a spur to the development of commercial capitalism and the expansion that came with it.

Nowhere in Asia at that time, except in Japan, was there a social system similar to feudalism in Europe. In Japan, the conditions for its liquidation developed during the Tokugawa period (1603-1868). Only the Meiji Restoration (1868), however, made a centralized nation out of an erstwhile feudal society; and appropriately it released Japan, only then, to a policy of expansion. Only then did Japan show what Western Europe began to show in the late Middle Ages: the capacity to organize war on at least a quasi-national (i.e., waningly feudal) basis. This was a capacity that helped to make those Middle Ages "later," harbingers of modern times. To equip armies and navies and defensive positions with cannon had demanded the consolidation of state power, the mobilization of technical, financial, and administrative resources. Then, expansion into the world could be achieved.

Back in Portugal, back at the beginnings of the new era, we see, in the next pair of extracts, the importance of social structure for the dynamic new developments.

The Rise of Maritime and Commercial Elements

In the absence of great natural or physical frontiers to protect them against aggression or absorption, the Portuguese were under the necessity of defending themselves by walls of living flesh against Muslim imperialism and, later, that of Castile; but in this very effort to make pure human resistance or tension supply the lack of almost any kind of geographic defense—any great river or mountain range—they availed themselves of the aid of foreigners. In the Crusades, as in the wars of independence, this was very evident, and this it is that explains not only Portuguese nationalism, which is practically without a geographic base, but Portuguese cosmopolitanism as well. A cosmopolitanism largely favored, it is true, by the geographic situation of the Kingdom: that of a prevailingly maritime country which from remote times has had a great variety of human contacts. On the one hand, it has received upon its shores successive waves, or, more frequently, driblets, of maritime peoples. On the other hand, its navigators, fishermen, and merchants have gone to foreign shores and foreign waters to do their fishing and their scenting-out of new markets.

It was not long after 1184, João Lúcio de Azevedo believes, that commercial relations between Portugal and Flanders must have begun, while those with England date from the opening years of the thirteenth century. And there were also "merchants who went to Levantine ports, designated in the language of the epoch as overseas ports." In the time of Dom Diniz, Portuguese vessels, some of them enormous for the period, of more than a hundred tons, were frequenting the northern ports and those of the Mediterranean. Porto intensified its maritime and mercantile activity, and in 1230 its burghers succeeded in getting themselves exempt from military service in connection with the conquest of Algarve by "contributing money for the purpose." From this it may be seen how precocious was the effect that a commercial cosmopolitanism was having upon the formation of Portuguese society. Cosmopolitanism and finance, a bourgeois mercantilism.

It is, thus, to the "non-Hispanic" elements, as Antônio Sérgio puts it, foreign elements of diverse origin, that we must attribute the failure of Castile to incorporate the western portion of the

From Gilberto Freyre, *The Masters and the Slaves: A Study in the Development of Brazilian Civilization* (New York: Alfred A. Knopf, 1946), pp. 194-96. © 1946 by Alfred A. Knopf, Inc. Reprinted by permission of the publisher. Footnotes omitted.

peninsula, "where the commerce of northern Europe met that of the Mediterranean." It was the foreign elements of the population at this dubious and impressionable point of confluence between northern and southern Europe and the Levant that were responsible for the dissemination of cosmopolitan and separatist, maritime and commercial tendencies, tendencies that soon were to evolve into impetuous forces making for differentiation and autonomy.

The precocious ascendancy of the maritime and commercial classes in Portuguese economy and politics was a result, likewise, of the extraordinary variety of seafaring and mercantile stimuli. In the beginning the great agents of differentiation and autonomy were the Crusaders, northern adventurers who, in the earldom of Portucale, set themselves up as a military and territorial aristocracy. One of them even became a founder of the monarchy. But this element was afterwards to form a conservative stratum, inclined out of economic class interest to a reunion with Castile. It was then that the differentiating and autonomist activity, and native or patriotic sentiment as well, came to be concentrated in the maritime and mercantile cities. In Lisbon. In Porto. Among the bourgeoisie and the popular classes. According to Alberto Sampaio and Antônio Sérgio, it is from the beginning of Portuguese national life that the antagonism between the commercial class of the maritime cities and the landed aristocracy of the center of the country really dates. As this economic-class antagonism grew sharper, accentuating the divergence between rural and seafaring interests, the kings, in a desire to free themselves of any kind of aristocratic pressure upon their royal power, were inclined to adopt a policy that favored the commercial bourgeoisie and the people of the cities. The laws promulgated by Dom Fernando in the way of protecting maritime commerce and encouraging naval construction; the support given to the Master of Avis against the territorial aristocracy; the conquest of Ceuta—all these are initiatives and movements that reflect the precocious ascendancy of the bourgeoisie in Portugal.

The Transformation of the Aristocracy

. . . Lisbon became the seaport where the commerce of the north of Europe met that of the south; it was due to this tendency towards maritime commerce and the concentration of attention on the seaports that the problem of peopling the southern part of

From Gilberto Freyre, *Brazil: An Interpretation* (New York: Alfred A. Knopf, 1945), pp. 14-16. © 1945 by Indiana University. Reprinted by permission of the publisher. Footnote omitted.

Portugal, where agriculture has always depended on expensive irrigation, began to be neglected at an early stage. Since the chief aim of European commerce at this time was, as everyone knows, the acquisition of oriental products, the Portuguese business men of Lisbon, some of them Jews or connected with Jews, took advantage of the geographical situation of their town and also of the fact that feudalism was not so powerful in Portugal as in other parts of Europe to become masters of the national policy and to transform it into a bold cosmopolitan, commercial, and at the same time imperial adventure, through scientific and quasi-scientific efforts to discover new routes for commerce, new lands and new markets to be exploited, and pagan populations not only to be converted into Christians but also to be subdued into Portuguese subjects or slaves. The King of Portugal himself became "the Merchant of Merchants" and the state officials also turned traders.

It is well known that in the fourteenth and fifteenth centuries, with the irruption of the Turks into the eastern seaports of the Mediterranean and because of other difficulties, the need for a sea-route to India became acutely felt in Europe. No European nation was in a more advantageous position to solve this grave problem than semi-European Portugal, a nation so precociously maritime and commercial in its political program that, as early as the latter part of the fourteenth century, laws were enacted by King Dom Fernando which gave special protection to maritime commerce and encouraged naval construction; which gave more assistance to such a cause than to the noble proprietors of latifundia, especially of lands regained from the Moors—lands that needed irrigation, then considered a matter of royal aid or something above the economic capacity of the not-too-wealthy proprietors. It seems that such aid was never given. In not assisting the aristocratic proprietors of latifundia, the kings of Portugal perhaps had in view the definite and efficient development of centralized royal power, which might be endangered by a strong land aristocracy.

The policy of disdain or neglect of the Portuguese hinterland followed by some of the most influential kings of Portugal like Dom Fernando explains why so many noblemen began to come to Lisbon as candidates for government appointments. And, as such, even they grew enthusiastic over maritime adventure, trade, naval construction; they became co-operators, rather than enemies, of the merchant princes of the seaports when the sea-route to India was opened and parts of the East became colonies or semi-colonies of Portugal.

V / CONCLUSION

The Confucian bureaucracy that smothered Cheng Ho and all that he might have represented was not a feudal class, and Chinese emperors, for all the Confucian-imperial tension, had a symbiotic relationship with the bureaucratic order. Each lived on the other, and neither nurtured a rising bourgeoisie.

We have suggested that in Chinese society the key to power was the combined possession of land and office in a tax-collecting, centralized state. This society was admirably served by Confucianism's traditionalism, its anti-legalist moral bias, its theory of free social mobility, and the premium it set on the mastery of a literary inheritance. It was a society in which the landed bureaucracy, by a combination of threat and lure, could always (before the catalytic intrusion of the nineteenth-century West) make abortive the revolutionary impulse in proto-capitalist elements, a society always open to rebellion or invasion but not to revolution. As Weber put it, successful usurpation of the throne or successful invasion simply meant a different tax-receiver, not an altered social order.

Ideally and logically, feudalism as a sociological "ideal type" is blankly opposed to capitalism. But historically and chronologically it gave it stimulation. The very absence of feudal restraints in China put a greater obstacle in the way of the expansion of capitalism (and capitalistic world-expansion) than their presence in Europe. For the non-feudal bureaucratic society of China, a self-charging, persisting society, just insofar as it was ideally more congenial than feudal society to elementary capitalist forms, accommodated and blanketed the embryonic capitalism, and ruined its revolutionary potential. Is it any wonder, then, that even in Portugal, one of the least of the capitalist powers in the end, a social process quite the reverse of China's should release the force of expansion instead of contracting it? It was a process, in Portugal and Western Europe generally, of a proto-capitalist extrication from feudalism and erosion of feudalism. And this was a process quite different from the persistence in China of a *non-feudal*, bureaucratic society, a depressant of feudalism—and of capitalism, too.

In technology, Europe came into early modern times perhaps better able to expand into the world; but Asians had a technology that was adequate to build on. In Asia's case it was a lack of the impulse to develop technologically to the fullest effect for expansion, not of a lack in technology to implement an impulse to expand.

In religion, the European crusading tradition was perhaps more conducive to expansion than Asian quietism; but Asian religions, especially Islam, had had their own ecumenical pretensions and proselytizing purposes. And Western Christian probes, as in the thirteenth- and fourteenth-century Far Eastern missions, had (in secular ways) encouraged, not exemplified, the general Western expansionist fervor.

In "spirit," Europe came to appear perhaps more boldly adventurous; but this is a factor notoriously hard to pin down. It is probably an impressionistic deduction from the fact—*after* the fact—of Europe's expansion, not an immanent condition of its occurrence.

Technology, religion, and spirit must be seen in a social matrix. The economic forces that burst the confines of feudal fragments, to integrate the nations and the world; the political forces that transcended feudal fragments, to create nations and burst into the world—these were Western forces, in alliance, that had feudalism behind them to nurture them to the point of superseding it, and to the point of carrying Europeans to Asian lands that lacked it.

24 / A SUMMARY FROM THE VANTAGE POINT OF EUROPE

Communication

The rapid communications which Europeans developed, and their

From Robert L. Reynolds, *Europe Emerges: Transition toward an Industrial World-wide Society, 600-1750*. (Madison: The University of Wisconsin Press, 1961), pp. 414-19. © 1961 by The Regents of the University of Wisconsin. Reprinted by permission of the publisher.

monopoly of communications, gave them an ability to know where to go, what to do, and how to do it, in a way no non-European people could match. European rapidity of communication was the astonishment of all the world when other peoples first met them. To this day it has been a specialty. European packet boats and clippers, then European telecommunications of every sort, up to high-speed airplanes, have given them a monopoly of communications most of the time, and almost a complete monopoly in the technology for improving communications.

European pre-eminence in this respect was greatly furthered by the invention of the movable-type printing press, which from just about 1450 on began to make it possible for one European to go somewhere, see something and describe it, and have any European who could read Latin (then the universal language) know all about it within a few weeks, thanks to the speedy circulation of printed materials.

Newsletters, then newspapers; scholarly letters, then scholarly journals; institutions organized and maintained permanently where trained men could gather and weigh and find meaning in reports and experiences touching geography, geology, climatology, zoology, botany, and so on—all these and many more things were factors in the rapid and exclusively European exploration of the earth.

Growing Global Monopoly in Trade

Europeans were excellent traders, far better than most others, although in no way more skilled than, say, the Arabs or Chinese in this respect.

In many parts of Europe, notably in Tuscany and Lombardy, Catalonia and France, in England, in the Low Countries, and in the developed southern and Rhineland parts of Germany, there were a great many men accustomed to working for their livings by using tools and raw materials. . . . Some of these made finished goods while others performed a single process in the step-by-step manufacture of a finished article, in working metals or textiles, as well as others. The skills of Europeans were matched by certain non-European specialists in different special fields, but in many given fields the former were generally better than the majority of the craftsmen of the rest of the world. While the Incas were better than Europeans in their work with some sorts of textiles, the Europeans were better cloth-makers than most other American Indians and many other peoples; while the Indians of India or the Chinese were better than Europeans in some sorts of brass work, still the

Europeans were better in this field than everyone else except the Indians and Chinese, to cite instances.

European traders themselves capitalized on the special skills of foreign peoples in two ways. In the East the people of India and China had no means of their own for selling their products to people any distance away, so soon after 1500 the Europeans built up a most profitable carrying trade, distributing the products of one place in the East to markets in other places. European ships and traders carried goods from Canton to Manila, to Calcutta, to Bombay, to Persia, to the islands of the South Seas. In return they carried all sorts of products from the places named (and literally hundreds of others) back to Canton. Through this carrying trade, the special skills and appetites of Far Eastern peoples furnished a most lucrative business to European traders, who were the only ones possessing both the ships and the knowledge of markets far away. As they came to monopolize the delivering of goods from one place to another, European ships and merchants could, if they wished, either handle those goods or not, as their interests led them.

Because of this monopoly, Europeans could capitalize on the special skills of special peoples in a second way: they could carry foreign articles with a tested profitable market home to Europe where skilled European workmen could learn to imitate them; once Europeans had begun manufacturing those articles, it was the European-produced goods which could be delivered to other parts of the world. They were in a fine position to push their materials and products in the world market, for they were the only ones who could carry materials and products.

For example, Europeans long prized the shawls which were made in the north of India in the Kashmir region; much later Scotchmen were making imitations of those shawls by the dozens per day; called "Paisley" shawls, they swept the Kashmir shawls off the general market. Europeans admired the very hard vitrified china of the Chinese, and for a long while bought it to sell to other peoples, taking it from China and distributing it. But then the Europeans began to make it in France and elsewhere, and shortly true Chinese china had become a rare article on the world market while Europe was making and selling enormous amounts of its own "china." For a good while Europeans bought cottons of a very fine quality from India for markets in Africa, Europe, and America, but before too long they had imitated them in England and were shipping cheaper machine-made cottons back to India where they ruined the Indian cotton-weaving industry in its own home.

European labor was relatively cheap, and became progressively cheaper as the first great wave of exploration and discovery swept on. It became progressively cheaper because of inflation, which raised prices faster than it raised wages. In the 1500s and 1600s the laborers in the textile industries, for example, were getting poorer in terms of real wages, which made the European cloths put out on the market of the world steadily lower in price as against prices for other things.

Furthermore, Europeans were endlessly experimenting with machinery. The great epoch for the application of water power and steam to the moving of heavy machinery was to come in the 1700s, but prior to that time Europeans constantly worked on improving mechanisms. Use of machinery further reduced the cost of labor in the making of a given item, and European goods tended to become less and less expensive.

The line of European goods was long, for they made all sorts of things on their own account. While in such places as India some kinds of iron and brass work might have been better, generally nobody could make such good copper or brass kettles, such good iron or steel tools, or such good implements for the hunter, housewife, or craftsman. Consequently, metal goods sold all about the globe tended to be of European manufacture. As Europeans came to any new area, their better metal goods came to dominate its economy, which became dependent upon further imports. The American Indians not only went over to use of French and Spanish iron and brass for their tools, they also forgot how to make stone tools. Only a generation after a tribe began to get a good supply, they had to have European tools or none. That brought dependence in many other respects.

Europeans were also very clever and seemingly had fun inventing all kinds of gewgaws which would amuse, interest, and please men and women in other parts of the world. Incidentally, Europeans liked these things too, and did not invent them just for foreigners. European dandies and ladies wore little tinkly bells on their clothes, little brass ornaments, and so on. They also invented good mirrors, and there is nothing which will sweep a virgin market so fast as a good mirror. Men love them. Anywhere the Europeans went, their mirrors with "silvering" on the back of good clear glass were a solid trade line. Cheap knives, spoons, bells, mirrors, were known as "trade goods."

Other excellent items were blankets and textiles of every sort. They came to have a good line of tobacco goods, not because tobacco was raised in Europe to any extent, but because they controlled the other parts of the world where it could be raised. They took the tobacco of Virginia, or Sumatra, or wherever it began to be grown (usually the Europeans began seeing that it was grown commercially) and sold it everywhere.

At a crucial moment the Europeans developed commercial distilling, so that they had distilled alcoholic beverages to sell. It was at or near the top of the European list. Most other peoples did not know how to make liquor, and it was always salable, and usually greatly facilitated sale of the rest of a line of goods. In business the first step normally was to give the customer a couple of good drinks, then to start talking.

European knowledge of how to gather large sums of capital and to manage such things as the great joint stock of the East India Company of England was tremendously important. Control of bookkeeping and of financial operations of all kinds, by a single man in one room, for an organization whose finances and books and affairs were spread over half the globe, was a European invention, something never before tried. Europeans were also very skilled in handling the financing of purchasing and selling all around the world. They were perspicacious when it came to sizing up those who could be trusted and those who could not, and clever at determining the amounts of discounts or charges which should be made. European knowledge of how to sell goods was never better than that of their nearest rivals, the Arabs and Chinese, but they went everywhere, while the Chinese went only to the Philippines, Indonesia, and Indochina. The Arabs lost leadership even in their home waters, and thereafter their ventures were never extended very far.

Return shipments from lands overseas were of the greatest importance also. For a European merchant it was those profits on the goods he brought home for sale that were his final ones. At home there was a great hunger for goods from abroad. China from the Chinese was in great demand until it could be duplicated and even improved on at home; embroideries and elegant articles for the luxury market were always in demand; desire for furs continued unabated, a demand which could be met with furs from either Siberia or the North American continent; and so on.

It was in the realm of food that one of the greatest changes in

European habits was to come; a demand for foreign food products steadily increased. There was always the old demand for the spices of the Spice Isles, and added to this there came to be a demand for some of the new spices from the Western Hemisphere. Some of the chili spices the Indians used became an important part of the diet in Spain, while importation of cayenne and other hot peppers became important for the general European market.

There was already a home market hungry for sugar. Development of sugar plantations, first in the Mediterranean, then in the Atlantic islands and finally the Western Hemisphere, afforded sugar supplies on a large scale. In addition, cocoa, coffee, and tea, products never before known in Europe, came to be liked very much. In general, these were tropical or semitropical products which could be carried to Europe not for cultivation but only for consumption.

The ever-widening diet possibilities which came with the introduction of foreign foods and beverages to the European market brought about a considerable change in eating and living habits. During the late 1500s and thereafter, the European diet became much more varied than it had ever been before. Artistic cookery began to be important in both Italy and France. In England the famous coffee houses became popular centers where gentlemen of fashion, politics, and wit gathered (as well as some of the racier and more disreputable types), while their ladies entertained their friends at China tea parties—both phenomena made possible by the importation of tea and coffee from abroad.

Integration of Government and Business

It was a great asset to the Europeans in commerce that European governments put their whole strength behind mercantile enterprise, and considered the devising of ways and means for making their merchants richer and stronger a valid activity. The most powerful foreign states with which European merchants came in contact may have been equal to the Europeans in warfare, but none of them was so helpful in the promotion of trade and of the merchant class. In fact, . . . Chinese, Japanese, Indians of India, and many others looked down upon their merchant classes. In general these peoples, who could match the Europeans in other ways, were indifferent to mercantile activity. Modern governments which foster trade are following a pattern established by the strong states of Europe some six or seven hundred years ago. Those

European governments had a theory that if their merchants were strong and rich, the governments themselves would carry greater weight in war and diplomacy.

During the 1400s the European world had developed a curious shortage of gold as compared with other metals and resources, and there was a hunger for it. This was not to last in that acute form forever, but when we read of the almost hysterical greed with which Spaniards and Portuguese approached a pile of gold, we must remember that it was far more valuable per ounce in terms of purchasing power than it had been before or than it has been in modern times. The gold fever of such men as Cortes and Pizzaro was something that drove men to exploration, stimulated their trading activities, and also stimulated them to conquest. Just at the time of Christopher Columbus's trip to the New World, the European money and price structure had gone somewhat out of equilibrium because of an imbalance between gold and silver, and of gold and silver against commodities. . . .

25 / A SUMMARY FROM THE VANTAGE POINT OF ASIA

The Western countries have shown a superiority complex by claiming themselves to be "developed" while degrading some other countries by calling them "under-developed." I do not agree with these terms. Now they promote the so-called underdeveloped countries by describing them as developing countries. So far as China is concerned, we are not grateful for that. The facts over the past three centuries show that the so-called developed countries have developed by exploiting the colonies, while the so-called underdeveloped countries remain undeveloped as a result of imperialist and colonialist exploitation. No rigid line should be drawn by classifying certain countries as developed and some others as underdeveloped. We hold that, politically, the Asian, African, and Latin American countries which persist in opposing imperialism and colonialism are advanced, while the West European and North American imperialist countries are backward. Economically, we do not believe that the people of Asia, Africa, and Latin America will for ever remain backward and that Western Europe and North America will for ever be in the van technically.

Quoted in "Chen Yi on China's Policies," *The Broadsheet* (London), II, No. 11 (November 1965), 3.

Chen Yi made this statement on September 29, 1965, as Vice-Premier and Foreign Minister of Communist China. "European expansion and the counter-example of Asia" is clearly a sensitive subject. The anti-imperialist Chen Yi starts with Europe's expansion and makes it the ground of Western development. And so, in large part, it was. But behind the expansion of Europe, behind the condition of Asia as "Counter-example," different paths of initial development had to be trod, to bring this book to its point of departure. All questions of conquest and exploitation aside, the dynamics of Western and Asian societies were different, and they made for different historical careers. All questions of static comparison aside—comparison at a movement in time, say 1450, that might have warranted speculation about Europe's lying open to Asia— no one, for the next five centuries at least, would be preparing a book on "Asian expansion and the counter-example of Europe."

BIBLIOGRAPHY

Since the aim of this book is not primarily to describe the great voyages or conquests, but to read back from them to the conditions of their taking place (or not taking place), we shall not canvass here the copious literature dealing directly with expansion out of Spain, England, China, etc., or with the careers of Western powers in Asia. Instead, we list some works in which technology, religion, or spirit (national or cultural character), dealt with in the context of social structure, are relevant to expansion or the abortiveness of expansion. Some of the works already cited in the text are more than illustrative: they are basic for this issue. Joseph Needham, *Science and Civilization in China*, seven volumes projected, Vols. I-IV (Cambridge, 1954-65) is one of these. For a brief statement of Needham's views, see his article, "Poverties and Triumphs of the Chinese Scientific Tradition" in a symposium volume that is highly suggestive for the subject of this book: A. C. Crombie, ed., *Scientific Change: Historical Studies in the Intellectual, Social and Technical Conditions for Scientific Discovery and Technical Invention, from Antiquity to the Present* (London, 1963). Both this volume and Lynn White, *Medieval Technology and Social Change* (Oxford, 1962) are more highly interpretive works than the series edited by Charles Singer, *A History of Technology*, five volumes (Oxford, 1954-58). A general work that includes technological development among its themes is Boies Penrose, *Travel and Discovery in the Renaissance, 1420-1620* (Cambridge, Mass., 1952).

There is a mountain of literature dealing with Christian evangelical impulses in the history of the expansion of Europe. One well-known work is C. R. Boxer, *The Christian Century in Japan, 1549-1650* (Berkeley, 1951). If expansion is related to the development of capitalism, then Max Weber, *The Protestant Ethic and the Spirit of Capitalism* (London, 1930) and its companion volume, *The Religion of China: Confucianism and Taoism* (Glencoe, Ill., 1951), R. H. Tawney, *Religion and the Rise of*

140

Capitalism (London, 1926), and the considerable literature of commentary on these works show other lines of approach to the factor of religion in expansion, and to the factor of "spirit." Is the broad distinction between Europe and Asia a distinction between economic spirits or national characters? G. F. Hudson, *Europe and China* (London, 1931) discusses, among many other things, the difference between Western aggressiveness and Chinese civility.

An example of a book dealing, not with the effect of religion on economic developments or *vice versa,* but with the combination of the two is W. L. Schurz, *The Manila Galleon* (New York, 1959). The emphasis is economic. Myron P. Gilmore, *The World of Humanism, 1453-1517* (New York, 1952) relates the commercial revolution of the sixteenth century to the overseas discoveries and dynastic consolidations. Capitalist developments were both causes and effects of expansion; the capitalist effects of the discoveries are emphasized in H. M. Robertson, *Aspects of the Rise of Economic Individualism* (Cambridge, 1933), a work which called forth a considerable literature of controversy. C. R. Boxer, in *The Dutch Seaborne Empire, 1600-1800* (London, 1965) dwells on a capitalist social and economic milieu which initially fostered an expansionist program. A particularly fine specimen of the literature on Chinese society relevant to the contrast between Confucian China and expansionist Europe, is Ping-ti Ho, *The Ladder of Success in Imperial China: Aspects of Social Mobility, 1368-1911* (New York, 1962). Part of this contrast can be glimpsed in Rushton Coulborn, ed., *Feudalism in History* (Princeton, 1956), which shows the background to the nation-building that released the forces of expansion.